EMMAUS BIBLE RESOURCES

C000063833

Missionary Journeys, Missionary Church

ACTS 13 – 20

EMMAUS BIBLE RESOURCES

The Lord is Risen! – Luke 24

Steven Croft

Also available:

Travelling Well

Stephen Cottrell and Steven Croft

EMMAUS BIBLE RESOURCES

Missionary Journeys, Missionary Church

ACTS 13 – 20

STEVEN CROFT

EMMAUS: THE WAY OF FAITH

The National Society
Leading Education
with a Christian Purpose
Church House Publishing

National Society/Church House Publishing
Church House
Great Smith Street
London SW1P 3NZ

ISBN 0 7151 4972 5

Published 2001 by National Society Enterprises Ltd

Tel: 020 7898 1557;
Fax: 020 7898 1449;
Email: copyright@c-of-e.org.uk.

Cover design by Church House Publishing

Typeset in Franklin Gothic and Sabon

Printed in England by The Cromwell Press Ltd,
Trowbridge, Wiltshire

Contents

How to use this book   vii

Introduction to **Emmaus Bible Resources**   ix

Acknowledgements   xi

An Introduction to Acts 13 – 20   1

Chapter 1   **There and Back Again – Acts 13 and 14**   7

First impressions – Acts 13 and 14   7
The place to begin – Acts 13.1-3   9
A miracle in Cyprus – Acts 13.4-12   11
The gospel to the Jews – Acts 13.13-43   12
Responding to the gospel – Acts 13.44 – 14.7   14
Homeward bound – Acts 14.8-28   17
Guidelines for groups (1)   19

Chapter 2   **Meetings, Meetings, Meetings! – Acts 15**   22

Conflict at the centre   22
Setting the scene – Acts 15.1-5   24
Debate in Jerusalem – Acts 15.5-21   25
The letter to the Gentiles – Acts 15.22-35   27
Acts and Galatians – Galatians 1 and 2   29
Farewell to Barnabas – Acts 15.36-41   31
Guidelines for groups (2)   34

Chapter 3   **Breaking New Ground – Acts 16.1 – 18.23**   36

New directions – Acts 16.1-10   36
New beginnings – Acts 16.11-15   38

Cry freedom! – Acts 16.16-40   40
Turning the world upside down – Acts 17.1-15   42
Preaching in Athens – Acts 17.16-34   44
To Corinth with love – Acts 18.1-23   47
Guidelines for groups (3)   49

Chapter 4   **The Last and the Greatest – Acts 18.24 – 20.12**   52

Setting the scene – Acts 18.24-28   52
Laying the foundation – Acts 19.1-7   55
The Hall of Tyrannus – Acts 19.8-10   57
Handkerchiefs and aprons – Acts 19.11-20   59
Riot in Ephesus – Acts 19.21-40   62
Consolidation – Acts 20.1-12   64
Guidelines for groups (4)   67

Chapter 5   **Over to You! – Acts 20.17-38**   69

Ministry in Acts – Acts 20.17-38   69
The Word made flesh – Acts 20.18-20 and 33-35   71
The tears of an evangelist – Acts 20.18-25   74
The tears of a pastor – Acts 20.25-35   76
The tears of a Christian community – Acts 20.36-38   78
The message of his grace – Acts 20.32   81
Guidelines for groups (5)   83

Liturgical Resources   85

Notes   93

Further Reading   94

Notes on the Order for Daily Prayer   95

An Order for Daily Prayer   96

How to use this book

The *Emmaus Bible Resources* can be used on your own, with a small group and with a whole church or group of churches (or any combination of the three).

On your own

Each chapter is divided into six parts ending with a short prayer or meditation.

You can use the studies as part of a daily time of Bible reading and prayer.

Or you can read the chapter with the biblical text at a single sitting.

A simple Order for Daily Prayer is provided at the back of the book.

With a small group

The group can be three friends, a husband and wife, an ongoing home group or one drawn together for these studies.

Each member of the group should read a chapter of this book and the biblical text between meetings.

At the end of each chapter, you will find a 'Guideline for groups'.

Each group will need a convenor to guide you through this material.

With the whole church

The material is designed so that a church or group of churches could use it as the basis of Sunday and midweek material for learning and discussion.

Five Sundays can be identified as appropriate for a series of sermons on Acts 13 – 20. Tables of readings and other resources are provided in the Liturgical Resources section at the end of the book.

Members of the congregation who wish to engage with the text for themselves can then be encouraged to read this book as a study guide alongside the sermon series. Those who wish to do so can also meet in small groups during the week.

Introduction to *Emmaus Bible Resources*

The two disciples walk along the road to Emmaus with Jesus, although they do not recognize him. As they walk together, Jesus interprets and opens the Scriptures to them. They have no books or texts with them but these disciples would already be familiar with many of the words of Scripture and would perhaps have learned them by heart.

From the earliest times, Christians have read the Scriptures on their own, together and in the company of the risen Christ. Every act of Christian worship has at its centre the public reading of the Bible, the word of God. Through reading and study of the Scriptures, our Christian faith is refreshed, strengthened, challenged and renewed. As Paul writes to Timothy:

> All scripture is inspired by God and is useful for
> teaching, for reproof, for correction, and for training
> in righteousness, so that everyone who belongs to
> God may be proficient, equipped for every good work
> (2 Timothy 3.16-17).

It is becoming harder to live as a Christian. Every Christian needs to live out the truth of their baptism: each one of us is called to Christian discipleship and Christian service according to the gifts God has given to us.

The *Emmaus Bible Resources* are offered as a way of encouraging individuals, small groups and congregations to engage with the text of Scripture in order that they may be built up and grow in Christian life, faith and service.

As with *Emmaus: The Way of Faith*, we have tried to combine sound and orthodox Christian theology with good educational practice on the one hand and a commitment to equip the whole Church for mission on the other.

Each book in the series is complete in itself and is intended as a guide either to a passage of Scripture or to a short series of passages grouped around a central theme. We hope to publish two or three books in the series each year. Normally the passage will be part of a longer book within the Bible, or it may be the whole of one of the shorter books.

Each book in the series is largely written by one person (whose name appears on the cover) but has been edited by the original group of authors. We hope, over time, to involve others outside the original group in developing new material for the series.

Each author has been asked to write for a general Christian audience but to bring to the work insights from the Christian tradition of interpretation and the best of contemporary biblical scholarship. Notes and references have been kept to a minimum although there are some ideas for further reading. Each book also encourages a variety of learning styles in terms of individual study and reflection and group interaction.

Wherever possible, some of the material in each book has been piloted both with individuals and in small groups. We are very grateful to the churches, groups and individuals who have assisted in this way. The new series can be used just as well by individuals and churches who have not used the original *Emmaus* material as by those who have been using it for many years.

Five years after the publication of *Emmaus: The Way of Faith*, we are surprised and humbled at the many ways God has used the material, through the ministry and prayers of many Christian people and for the building up of Christians, of churches and, ultimately we pray, of the kingdom of God. Our prayer for this new series is that it may be used by God in similar ways and to the same ends.

Stephen Cottrell
Steven Croft
John Finney
Felicity Lawson
Robert Warren

Acknowledgements

Some of the material here in Chapters 4 and 5 was first presented in the form of sermons preached in St George's, Ovenden, Halifax, in 1995 and the preparatory material for the studies was presented as Bible Readings in Cranmer Hall in the autumn of 2000. The material in Chapter 3 was piloted by members of the first Ely Diocesan Lay Conference at Caister in March 2001. The author is grateful to the organizing group and to the members of the conference for constructive feedback on these sections.

The publisher gratefully acknowledges permission to reproduce copyright material in this book. Every effort has been made to trace and contact copyright holders. If there are any inadvertent omissions, we apologize to those concerned and undertake to include suitable acknowledgements in all future editions.

Unless otherwise indicated, the prayers and reflections at the end of each section of text are by the author.

Bible quotations are from *The New Revised Standard Version of the Bible* copyright © 1989 by the Division of Christian Education of the National Council of Churches in the USA. All rights reserved.

Extracts from *Common Worship: Services and Prayers for the Church of England* (Church House Publishing, 2000) are copyright © The Archbishops' Council of the Church of England.

'Spirit of the Living God' by Paul Armstrong is copyright © 1984 Restoration Music Ltd/Sovereign Music UK, PO Box 356, Leighton Buzzard, LU7 3WP, UK. Reproduced by permission (p. 56).

'Be Thou My Vision' is from *The Poem Book of the Gael* translated by M.E. Byrne and edited by Eleanor Hull. Originally published by Chatto & Windus. Reprinted by permission of The Random House Group Limited © the Estate of Eleanor Hull (p. 61).

An Introduction to Acts 13 – 20

Introducing Acts

The book of Acts is the most exciting and dramatic book in the New Testament. As we read it, we are gripped by the unfolding story of the spread of the Christian gospel from Jerusalem where the story begins to ancient Rome where it ends. We find accounts of the early disciples empowered to speak and to work miracles; of thousands converted to Christianity; of the continuous growth of the Early Church even as it wrestles with serious questions of doctrine and practice. On the way we glimpse how the message of Jesus Christ affects individuals, families and whole cities. We see the Christian Church prevailing even under the most vigorous persecution, facing setback after setback.

We continue our journey with characters we have come to know from the gospels, especially Peter and John. We are introduced to a range of new disciples who take major and minor roles: Barnabas, Lydia, Priscilla and Aquila and, most prominently, to the apostle Paul. We see Christians in their homes and home-based churches. We see them in the temple; at prayer; in prison and under house arrest; speaking sometimes just to one person and sometimes to great crowds. We are taken on a guided tour of the Roman world, visiting small towns and great cities, islands and new continents, travelling both by land and by sea. We witness the establishing of early Christian ministry, both its principles and its practice.

Throughout Christian history, men and women have returned to the book of Acts to find their faith and ministry renewed and rekindled: to be set on fire again for the gospel. As we read today we are caught up in the drama of the Christian life. Is this how things are meant to be? How are we to understand these things? Can the Christian Church regain in our own generation this same confidence, zeal and strength which so marks this account of the first Christian churches?

Introducing Luke

The book of Acts is written by the same author as the Gospel of Luke. Acts begins where Luke ends, with a similar dedication to someone called Theophilus, referring back to the gospel story.

> In the first book, Theophilus, I wrote about all that
> Jesus did and taught from the beginning until the day
> when he was taken up to heaven . . . (Acts 1.1-2).

The author presents most of his story as a narrator looking back on events at which he wasn't himself present but in some later sections, as we shall see, he writes as though he is himself a witness and a participant in the scenes he describes. He writes in the style of an ancient historian. In different parts of the book he is using different sources, including possibly eyewitness accounts. As in the gospel, Luke weaves these sources together very skilfully into a clear, well- ordered narrative which from earliest times was recognized by the Christian Church as being 'God-breathed' and part of holy Scripture.

The shape of the book

The book as a whole falls into three parts, which are carefully dovetailed together through overlapping some material. In Part 1 (chapters 1 – 12) we read the story of the Early Church based in Jerusalem beginning from the time of the Ascension of Jesus. We read of the gift of the Spirit on the day of Pentecost; of the establishing of the church in Jerusalem; of the quality of life among the believers and of the early and growing persecution, culminating in the death of Stephen, the first martyr. The gospel begins to spread further afield, carried by the early Jewish converts and Christian evangelists.

Luke prepares the way for the second and third sections of the book by telling us of the conversion of Saul (who is later known as Paul). Finally we read of the way in which, by God's grace, the gospel begins to spread beyond the Jewish community to the non-Jews (or Gentiles) beginning with Cornelius, a Roman centurion or army officer. A major centre of the Christian faith is established in the port and provincial capital of Antioch, where the disciples are first called 'Christians' (Acts 11.26).

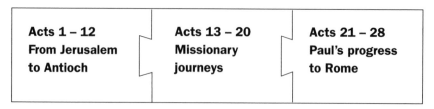

Acts 1 – 12	Acts 13 – 20	Acts 21 – 28
From Jerusalem	Missionary	Paul's progress
to Antioch	journeys	to Rome

In the second main section, which is our focus in this book, the spotlight is on Paul and his companions through three cycles of missionary activity: the first in the island of Cyprus and the area we know as modern Turkey; the second on mainland Greece and the third based in the large city of Ephesus which becomes a strategic centre for the gospel and one of the early centres of Christianity in the ancient world.

The final section of the book again takes a very different theme. In chapter 21, we follow Paul to Jerusalem where he is arrested and put on trial. In the remaining chapters we follow Paul's journey in captivity from Jerusalem to the city of Rome where tradition says he was later martyred for his faith. However, the final scene of the book is Paul again preaching the Christian gospel to the local leaders of the Jews. Luke ends his story on a note of hope:

> [Paul] lived there two whole years at his own expense
> and welcomed all who came to him, proclaiming the
> kingdom of God and teaching about the Lord Jesus
> Christ with all boldness and without hindrance
> (Acts 28.30-31).

Why was Acts written?

Christians through the ages have reflected on Luke's reasons for writing Acts. None of the other gospel writers (as far as we know) felt any need to continue the gospel story beyond the resurrection of Jesus. Clearly in Luke's mind there is a tremendous story to be told for its own sake.

As far as we can tell today, Luke was a careful historian as well as a master storyteller. He takes care with his language to use the proper terms for Roman cities and officials. What we read in Acts checks out against what we know of the towns and cities of the empire and conditions at the time. We would know from secular historians of the day how rapidly the Christian faith spread from its small beginnings in Judaea to every part of the civilized world even if Luke had never written his accounts.

But like all ancient historians and storytellers, Luke weaves his narrative so as to emphasize certain truths which Luke himself and the Church in which he wrote believed to be important for his own day and possibly for Christians in every generation. There is an overwhelming sense of encouragement for the Church running through Acts. Despite terrible setbacks and continual persecution, the fledgling Christian community not only survives but is enabled to grow and develop in ways it could not have imagined. There is a continuing stress on the grace, guidance and initiative of God in the progress of the gospel and particularly upon the power of the Holy Spirit in the mission of the Church. Luke is sensitive to the charges made against the Christian Church in his own day by those who were its enemies: charges that Christianity was automatically disruptive to Roman rule and order; caused civil unrest or disloyalty to the emperor. He takes particular care, as we shall see, to demonstrate that riot and disturbance are not caused directly by the Christians themselves but by those who are opposed to the gospel for a variety of reasons. The Christian faith itself is presented as reasonable, attractive and true to people of many different racial, cultural and social backgrounds, including Roman officials of various kinds. It is possible that part of the book was originally prepared as material for Paul's trial in Rome. There is a real possibility that the book of Acts itself saved thousands of Christians from a martyr's death.

Luke is also concerned in his own day to record carefully the ways in which the Christian community makes the gigantic leap from being a small sect within the Jewish faith to becoming a community open to men and women of every racial background and social and economic class. Perhaps most importantly in our own day, Luke is concerned to pass on the lessons from the period of the greatest missionary expansion of the Church to Christians of every generation. He is saying to us: 'This is what we saw; this is how we went about the business of communicating faith, making disciples and establishing new churches; these are the lessons we learned along the way. It was hard for us, but we saw tremendous fruit for the gospel and we knew difficulty but we also knew great joy. Read what we did and saw. Learn the lessons and apply them in your own church in your own day and see what God will do.'

The shape of this book

Our own study begins in **Chapter 1** with the story of the first missionary journey from Antioch and back to Antioch (Acts 13 and 14). The section contains the first of three major speeches by Paul in Acts 13 – 20, presenting the Christian gospel to a Jewish audience.

In **Chapter 2**, we examine the way in which the early Christians sought to resolve the major conflict which threatened to divide them: how to incorporate Jews and non-Jews within the same community (Acts 15). As we look at their conflict, we will try and learn some lessons for divided Christian communities today.

In **Chapter 3**, we look at the story of the great mission to Greece told in Acts 16, 17 and 18. We visit the great and very different cities of Philippi, Athens and Corinth among others. This section contains the second major speech, Paul's presentation of the gospel to a cultured Gentile audience in Athens.

In **Chapter 4,** we look at the last and the greatest of Paul's city-wide missions in the great centre of Ephesus where all the lessons of previous experience were applied and bore fruit (Acts 19). We will seek to learn some lessons for the Church of today.

Finally in **Chapter 5,** we examine Paul's great address to the elders of the church in Ephesus, the third major speech of the narrative. Paul looks back over his ministry in the city and passes on to the Christians there the responsibility for continuing the work in the same way. We will try and learn some lessons for the ministry and life of every Christian from the model Paul supplies.

Almighty God,
you called Luke the physician,
whose praise is in the gospel,
to be an evangelist and physician of the soul:
by the grace of the Spirit
and through the wholesome medicine of the gospel,
give your Church the same love and power to heal;
through Jesus Christ your Son our Lord. Amen.

Common Worship: Collect for Luke the Evangelist

Chapter 1

There and Back Again – Acts 13 and 14

First impressions – Acts 13 and 14

The story begins and ends in the great Christian centre at Antioch. Called by God, Barnabas and Saul are sent out in mission and travel through Cyprus and parts of modern Turkey. They see men and women converted. They meet opposition of different kinds. New Christian communities are established. Then the apostles return by the same route they went out, encouraging the new disciples and appointing elders in each church. The section ends as it began in Antioch, with Paul and Barnabas telling the story of all that God had done with them.

Try to get a sense of the flow of this great journey out and back again by reading through the two chapters at a single sitting. To give you a sense of the geography, mark the route of the journey on the map.

You'll find movement of some kind in the following verses:

- 13.1
- 13.4,5,6
- 13.13,14
- 13.51
- 14.6
- 14.20,21
- 14.24,25,26

The journey was under ancient, not modern conditions. The whole distance covered is just under 1,400 miles (2,240 kilometres). Slightly under half of the journey would be by sea under sail. The remainder would be by land on horseback or, most probably, by foot. Travel and communication in the Roman world was good by ancient standards, but still hazardous and difficult by modern reckoning. Barnabas and Paul had neither a Barclaycard nor a mobile phone in case of difficulty. They would be provided with some resources by the sending church in Antioch.

For much of the time however, they would be trusting to God and to the hospitality of the people they met. The account of their travels can be read in just a few minutes, but they would have taken several years to complete. This is an epic journey. Luke has given us highlights, perhaps using as his source an account written and preserved in the church in Antioch.

For hundreds of years of years before the time of Jesus, the Jewish people had been dispersed throughout the ancient world. For the most part, the Jews formed smaller communities of faith within the majority of towns and cities, centred on the synagogue, or place of worship. This Jewish community was the natural starting point for the mission of the apostles, since the Christian faith had begun among the Jews.

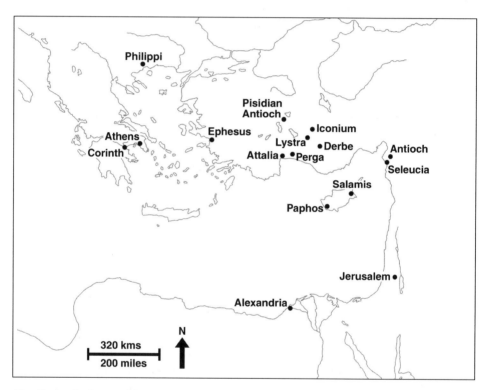

The first missionary journey

We see here that Paul and Barnabas' main strategy was to attend worship at the synagogue in each city they visited. As travelling teachers, they would be encouraged to speak, giving them a natural opportunity to talk of Jesus. The response in each city varies, but often at least some of the Jewish community reject the message of the apostles and they then move on to speak to the Gentiles. In this way, in each place, a small core of believers is established. This is the strategy we will see repeated over and over again in this part of Acts.

Take a moment to think about and write down your first impression of the two chapters. Is there a common theme? What strikes you most powerfully? Do you find them easy or difficult to read? What do you find hard to understand? What do they have to say to the Church today?

God of grace,
who called the apostles to leave their home
and preach the gospel to Jew and Gentile,
give to your church today the same courage,
love and faithfulness
as we tell of your love in this our generation.
through Jesus Christ, our Lord. Amen.

The place to begin – Acts 13.1-3

These few verses open a fascinating window onto the life of the early church in Antioch. To find out more about the foundation of this community look back to Acts 11.19-30. The city of Antioch itself was at this time a thriving metropolis. The church there was only recently established with a small number of able leaders and, no doubt, much work still to be done to consolidate the first Jewish and Gentile congregation.

There are five named and recognized Christian ministers called here 'prophets and teachers' (Acts 13.1). The brief descriptions indicate different racial and cultural backgrounds. At least one, possibly two, are black. At least one, Manaen, has a responsible day job as steward to the king. Paul's normal practice, as we shall see, was to earn his living as a tentmaker. Acts and the rest of the New Testament demonstrate that different titles emerge for recognized Christian ministers in different places. Clearly, however, there is the implication that ministry is a shared enterprise, exercised by a small but diverse group of people whose gifts have been recognized by the community: it is not the preserve of just one or two individuals.

The great missionary journey described in Acts 13 and 14 springs out of this fledgling Christian community in Antioch and its leaders. Note that it doesn't begin with a planning meeting or a report or a strategy document or any kind of human initiative. It begins with Christian people 'worshipping the Lord and fasting' (Acts 13.2). Just as in Acts 2, the disciples are 'all together in one place' on the day of Pentecost (Acts 2.1), so here the Christians in Antioch are deliberately seeking God. Fasting is not described frequently in Acts – only in this passage – although it is a discipline well known in the Old Testament and to the Jews of Jesus' day. Together with the worship of the church it signifies a particular desire to seek God's will for this Christian community. We should picture not a single event but probably a season in the life of the church in Antioch which is dedicated to seeking God's will for the next stage of its life.

Just as in Acts 2, God responds with a clear call to mission: 'the Holy Spirit said, "Set apart for me Barnabas and Saul for the work to which I have called them"' (Acts 13.2). For the present, Barnabas is the senior partner in the enterprise. The phrase 'the Holy Spirit said' occurs frequently in Acts. What lies behind the words here is probably a prophetic word given by one or more of those who are worshipping and fasting which is discerned by the whole community to be of God. This is God's initiative. The young church must give up its most senior leader in Barnabas, who came to them from Jerusalem itself, and its most gifted teacher, Saul. Paul uses the same word 'set apart' to describe his own calling in Romans 1.1. These two must go where God calls them. There is a readiness and an eagerness to answer God's call.

At some cost to the two individuals themselves and to the church, they are sent off. This time the mission's dependence upon the grace of God is emphasized by three things: fasting, and prayer and laying on of hands. We must assume that the congregation's support for those sent out continued whilst they were away so that the whole church shares in the missionary enterprise, although only a small group go physically.

The journey which Barnabas and Saul undertake will change their lives and have far-reaching effects for the kingdom. As we begin the journey with them, it is worth reflecting for a moment upon the readiness of the young Christians in Antioch to listen for God's call to them and their congregation and the readiness of Barnabas and Saul to respond. Are you clear in your own mind about God's call to you at the present time? When was the last time you set aside a season to attend to God through worship and through fasting, by means of a retreat or a quiet day, in order to be affirmed in your calling or allow God to move you on? Is there a need, with others, to take stock and follow the example of the Christians in Antioch?

God of the lost, the lonely and unloved,
in our weakness you call us still to serve you:
open our ears to hear your voice,
open our eyes to the needs of the world,
set us apart for the work to which you call us;
may we answer with your servant,
'Lord, here am I, send me.'

A miracle in Cyprus – Acts 13.4-12

Again Luke emphasizes that the disciples are 'sent out by the Holy Spirit' (Acts 13.4) rather than simply by the church. They travel to the sea and then cross to Cyprus, a journey of about 60 miles (100 kilometres). No mention is made of where Barnabas and Saul are expected to go in their travels. However, Barnabas is from Cyprus and so there is a logical reason for their moving in this direction. John is mentioned as a helper to prepare the way in 13.13 and 15.37. Nothing significant seems to happen for the majority of their stay on the island. There is no indication as to whether the early part of the preaching tour is fruitful or not.

However, in Paphos, seat of the Roman proconsul, Luke takes time to narrate in some detail the encounter with the magician or Jewish false prophet named Bar-Jesus or Elymas. The story can be read at a number of different levels. The first is as a simple account of a miracle accompanying the preaching of the gospel. There are a number of these all the way through Acts, as we shall see. From the day of Pentecost onwards, miraculous signs of different kinds were a feature of the early Christian preaching. We should not be ashamed of them or surprised when we encounter them, particularly among those who are coming new to the faith. Sergius Paulus is a real figure from history. Both he and his family feature in a number of inscriptions from the time.

At the second level, the story offers a number of fascinating contrasts between Sergius Paulus and Elymas on the one hand and between Elymas and Paul on the other. Sergius Paulus demonstrates one kind of response to the gospel. He is an 'intelligent man' who 'wanted to hear the word of God' (Acts 13.7). After listening to Paul and Barnabas and seeing what happened to Elymas, he believed. Elymas demonstrates a different response based on opposition to the faith, most probably jealous of anyone who might exert influence over the proconsul. Because of his response, Elymas is afflicted with physical blindness to match his inability to see spiritual things. A few chapters earlier, Paul himself was struck blind after his vision of the risen Christ. Here, Elymas' blindness leads to spiritual sight for someone else.

Finally, at the third level, Sergius Paulus is a type in the story not only of Roman officials who occur frequently in Acts but of educated Romans as a whole (of whom Theophilus was probably one). The proconsul, like all such educated Romans, is offered a choice. One the one hand, there is superstition and magic lacking in any real authority, signified by Elymas. On the other hand, there is the new Christian faith, building upon the foundation laid by Judaism yet open to all, with its gospel of the forgiveness of sins in Christ, with its preaching supported by learned arguments and by miracles. The old Roman religion had reached the end of its life. Which of the new alternatives would the educated person now choose?

For reflection

In your experience, who are the people in your world who are most likely to want to learn more about the Christian gospel? Who are the people most likely to resist the Christian message? Make a note of both groups and pray for them.

> In the tender compassion of our God
> the dawn from on high shall break upon us,
> To shine on those who dwell in darkness and the
>   shadow of death,
> and to guide our feet into the way of peace.

Common Worship: from the Benedictus, Luke 1.78,79

The gospel to the Jews – Acts 13.13-43

It is not entirely clear why the apostles travel inland to Antioch in Pisidia from Cyprus. There is some evidence that the family of Sergius Paulus had connections in the region and also that Paul may have moved away from the coast because of an illness. The New Testament letter to the Galatians was written to the churches of this region a few years after the events described here. In the letter Paul writes: 'You know that it was because of a physical infirmity that I first preached the gospel to you' (Galatians 4.13). Antioch in Pisidia is over 3,000 feet (1,000 metres) above sea level. It may be that the companions turned inland seeking a healthier climate.

The apostles' strategy of preaching first to the Jews is outlined in detail here. As visiting Jewish teachers, the apostles are invited to speak at the synagogue in the city. Luke sets in the narrative his first example of Paul's preaching to a Jewish congregation. Like all the speeches in Acts (and in other ancient history writing) we should not read the words as an exact account of what was said but as the best kind of summary of all of Paul's preaching to his own people. In the way Acts is set out, the speech is similar to and in parallel with Peter's great speech to the Jews on the day of Pentecost. Many of the points made are the same. Luke is demonstrating to his readers that the two apostles proclaim the same gospel.

As you read the speech, notice a simple threefold structure. Paul first retells part of Israel's story. We hear of the rescue of the Israelites from Egypt, of the conquest of Canaan, the judges, Samuel, and then the kings Saul and David. No doubt this section of the speech would have been much longer and more detailed in real life. Paul is following the pattern of Jewish preaching, continually retelling the story of what makes the Jewish nation special. In modern language, he is connecting with his audience. As Luke gives these summaries of Israel's history throughout Acts, his is also consciously teaching the history of Israel to Gentile Christians (including ourselves). You will find a much longer 'history lesson' in Stephen's speech in Acts 7.

At the centre of Paul's speech, from verses 23 to 37, is the telling of another story: the story of Jesus. This is the heart of Peter's preaching and of Paul's: the announcing of the good news of Jesus Christ. As in the four gospels, most of the attention is focused on the beginning of the story (John the Baptist) and on the end (the trial, death and resurrection of Christ). The Jews had waited for many years for the coming of the Messiah, the Son of David. The prophecies about him would be well known and often spoken of in the synagogues. Paul takes great care, therefore, to say that everything which happened to Jesus is in fulfilment of the Old Testament Scriptures. As in the dialogue on the road to Emmaus, as in the story of Philip and the Ethiopian in Acts 8, the death and resurrection of Jesus is shown to be the fulfilment of Scripture and the heart of the Christian message.

In 1 Corinthians 15 Paul gives a very short summary of his own preaching of the gospel:

> For I handed on to you as of first importance what
> I in turn had received: that Christ died for our sins
> in accordance with the scriptures, and that he was
> buried, and that he was raised on the third day in
> accordance with the scriptures (1 Corinthians 15.3-4).

This is the centre of the good news of the Christian faith. The final section of the speech (Acts 13.38-41) emphasizes the offer of forgiveness of sins through the death and resurrection of Christ and a warning that those who reject the offer will find themselves in fulfilment of a different kind of prophecy.

For Christians reading Paul's speech today, we are given a chance to check the beginning and the centre of our Christian faith against the measure Luke provides here. The message is the same in every generation. The starting point for our Christian journey is the story of the death and resurrection of Christ: 'through this man forgiveness of sins is proclaimed to you' (Acts 13.38). All too often, the profound yet simple message of the gospel slips from the centre of our faith. We replace the message of grace, God's gift to us in Christ, with an empty religion of involvement in church, finding a role for ourselves, ritual instead of living faith. The way back is always the same: repentance and faith; inviting the risen Christ to be once again Lord of our lives. The sermon given in Antioch still speaks today to those who will listen.

> Lord Jesus, crucified,
> through your death my sins are forgiven.
> Lord Jesus, risen from death,
> through your life I am set free.

You may like to pray this prayer for some time, in the rhythm of breathing.

Responding to the gospel – Acts 13.4 – 14.7

The immediate response to Paul's sermon in Antioch is positive. People want to hear more and many become followers of Paul and Barnabas, both those who are Jews by birth and those who had converted to Judaism (who would be part of every synagogue). A process of teaching, encouragement and nurture begins.

But this is not the only response the gospel provokes. As you read through the passage, make a note in the table (or in a notebook) of the different reactions to what would be the same message at Antioch and in Iconium.

13.43 Many Jews and devout converts . . .	
13.44 Almost the whole city . . .	
13.45 The Jews . . .	
13.48 The Gentiles . . .	
13.50 The Jews . . .	
14.1 A great number . . .	
14.2 The unbelieving Jews . . .	
14.4 . . .	

How would you summarize the different responses? Which ones do you see most often today? We will see these and still other reactions as we read on through Acts.

How do the apostles themselves react to this range of responses to their message? Those who become believers are carefully encouraged and nurtured in their new faith. They are not daunted or deterred by the opposition, which is initially limited to counter-arguments (13.45) and then escalates to physical violence (13.50 and 14.19).

However, Paul and Barnabas clearly recognize a point when they have done all they can and further attempts to preach to a particular group or in a particular place become counterproductive. In Antioch there is a solemn moment at which they turn from the Jewish community to the Gentiles, again establishing Scripture as their authority. When the persecution grows worse still, they recognize for the first time the need to move on physically, leaving behind them a young group of believers. The prophetic action of shaking the dust off the feet echoes the instructions of Jesus to the 70 disciples in Luke 10.10-11:

> But whenever you enter a town and they do not
> welcome you, go out into its streets and say, 'Even
> the dust of your town that clings to our feet, we wipe
> off in protest against you.'

As in the early part of Acts, the attempt by the enemies of the gospel to drive out those who preach it only results in the message spreading to new places and the Christian faith growing still stronger.

In reflecting on different responses to the gospel message, modern readers need to pause and take care not to associate 'the Jews' of the book of Acts or of the gospel accounts of Jesus' Passion too closely with the Jewish people of today. In the early days of the Christian faith, there was clearly much animosity between the two groups and Acts portrays this as being initiated by the Jews. However, in the two thousand years that have followed Acts, it is the Jews who have been persecuted in terrible ways. On many occasions, the persecution has been at the hands of Christians, who have used the passages about opposition in the Scriptures as a justification for oppression and persecution of those who are still seen in the New Testament Scriptures as the people of God.

The persecution of the Jews has been a great evil and is an enormous stain on the history of the Christian Church. We need to take care as we read the book of Acts today not to associate the Jews of Paul's day with any Jewish people we may know where our call must be first to understand, befriend and build bridges between our different communities. Only then will it be possible to speak honestly and truthfully of our different understanding of Jesus and of the Messiah.

As we read the text today, we are reminded that the progress of the Christian gospel, and the Christian life in general, is not meant to be easy. We will meet difficulties as well as easy situations, sorrow as well as joy. On several occasions, Paul draws our attention in his letters to his sufferings for the sake of the good news he bears, some of which are described in this section of Acts (see 1 Corinthians 4.9-13; 2 Corinthians 4.7-12 and 11.22-29). The Christian way is rarely comfortable. Whatever the obstacles and difficulties in our own lives, we should ask God for the grace to persevere.

> I bind unto myself today
> The power of God to hold and lead,
> His eye to watch, his might to stay,
> His ear to hearken to my need.
> The wisdom of my God to teach,
> His hand to guide, his shield to ward;
> The word of God to give me speech,
> His heavenly host to be my guard.
>
> From the hymn, 'St. Patrick's Breastplate'
> translated by Mrs C.F. Alexander

Homeward bound – Acts 14.8-28

The story of Paul and Barnabas in Lystra contains the delightful and dramatic account of the apostles being mistaken for the Greek gods Zeus and Hermes. The picture Luke paints is one of simple and superstitious country people. We know from other writers that there were legends of the gods appearing in this region in this way. Clearly there are language barriers, which add to the confusion. Note how Luke uses irony. The crowds cry out: 'The gods have come down to us in human form' (Acts 14.11). Paul and Barnabas are indeed proclaiming that God became human but not in the way the crowds intend. Not for the last time, a riot or disturbance, which might have been blamed on the Christians, is put down to other causes.

When Barnabas and Paul hear of the crowd's intent, they demonstrate clearly and decisively that they do not welcome their actions. Luke records a speech meant to be taken as typical of the apostles' preaching to uneducated Greeks (who made up the bulk of the population of this part of the Roman Empire). We will hear Paul's speech to the educated pagans in chapter 17. Again, the apostles engage with where the audience are: in this case trapped in superstition and the worship of false gods. The words are designed to set people free from their misconceptions about God so they might begin a new search for him. We hear nothing, therefore, about Jesus Christ. In the apostles' preaching, that would come later.

Events in Lystra end in great violence. Paul is stoned and left for dead, yet still the journey continues to one further city. In Derbe we read that 'they made many disciples' (Acts 14.21). We must assume that the pattern of the mission was the same as the one already established. At that point the apostles begin to retrace their steps, taking a longer route back to their starting point in order to build up the young churches. In each place they 'strengthened the souls of the disciples and encouraged them to continue in the faith, saying, "It is through many persecutions that we must enter the kingdom of God"' (Acts 14.22). As so often, the apostles' own lives demonstrate the truth of their message.

The methods of evangelism and church planting used by Paul and Barnabas are different from the methods used by most of the Church in its missionary work since that day. It simply is not possible for the apostles to stay long in any centre at this stage in the mission. The new converts are established in the basics of the faith and are encouraged to persevere. Elders are appointed within each church, with prayer and fasting (echoing the way in which the apostles themselves were sent out in 13.3). Local leadership is seen to be essential. We will gain some impression of the instruction given to the ministers when we come to Acts 20.

From that point on however, the young churches are in God's hands. Both the apostles and the new converts need to rely upon the Holy Spirit and the gifts which are already present in the churches. Paul or Barnabas, or occasionally another itinerant minister, would visit from time to time. We know that Paul at least maintained a vigorous correspondence with the new congregations and the letters which he wrote to them form part of the New Testament today.

Then, Luke tells us, this journey ends in the place it began. The apostles return to Antioch. As the whole church has shared in the support of the mission, so now 'they called the church together and related all that God had done with them, and how he had opened a door of faith for the Gentiles' (Acts 14.27).

Beginning any new enterprise is relatively easy. There is enthusiasm, the attraction of new things and new people and, perhaps, some early success. Keeping going in the tough middle period of a project, a job or a Christian ministry is more demanding. Setbacks must be overcome. Opposition and resistance must be dealt with. There is a need for grit and determination and sheer perseverance.

But ending a task or a mission well is possibly the hardest of the three. Knowing when to stand back and let others take responsibility is not easy. Entrusting the outcome of so much hard work and prayer to others and to God demands particular resources of faith. Laying down a task that has formed much of your life and your identity, without knowing what will come next, presents new challenges in discipleship and Christian growth. Paul and Barnabas are able to do all of this, and return and rest in the place where the mission began. In our own lives, do we have the grace, strength and enthusiasm for the middle and the ending of a task as for its beginning?

Lord God,
maker and sustainer of all things,
give us grace and strength
not only to begin new projects
but to continue them faithfully
and to know how to draw them to a close
for the sake of your Son,
who calls all people to a life of love and praise. Amen.

Guidelines for groups (1)

This section at the end of each chapter gives guidelines for a 90-minute meeting of a small Bible study group of up to a dozen people. You could also use the material as a guide for a much smaller group of two or three friends or family members (in which case the timings may be different). The guidelines assume that the group members have looked at the Bible passages before the meeting and, ideally, have read through the reflections in this chapter. This session envisages taking the whole of the passage (two chapters) for discussion. Some of the later sessions will take shorter passages.

The guidelines are in three parts.

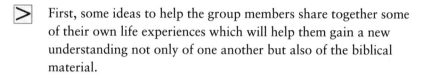

First, some ideas to help the group members share together some of their own life experiences which will help them gain a new understanding not only of one another but also of the biblical material.

Secondly, some questions for discussion which aim either take you further in understanding the Bible or help you reflect on its lessons for life today.

Finally, there are some practical ideas of things to discuss or to do in the light of each study. In a larger group, you should break down into smaller huddles of three or four people for some of the sections.

Approximate timings are given at the start of each section. However small your group, you would be wise to appoint someone as a facilitator to guide you through the discussion. Feel free to pick and choose the most helpful questions and to develop your own material. You will not have time to cover every question in any section. In order to keep a balance and shape to your meetings, it is more important to give time to at least one question from each section.

Give some thought in advance to where you might meet, the arrangement of the room and food and drink. Pray together in a way which is right for the group. No specific guidelines are given for this but you may want to use some of the prayers in the text or ideas from the liturgical section.

Sharing together (20 mins)

1. If this is a new group meeting, on the first occasion each person should take a moment to introduce themselves.

2. Each member of the group should say something about their hopes for your meetings together to discuss Acts 13 to 20. Ask everyone to give their initial impressions from Acts 13 and 14 and the study material. If you can, share one thing you gained and one question you bring.

3. What experience have members of the group had in acting as representatives on behalf of someone else either in the family or at work or in a voluntary capacity?

4. Allow time for each person to describe an experience of attempting to witness to your Christian faith either personally or as part of a group. How did it come about? What was the response? What were your reflections afterwards?

Studying together (50 mins)

1. Take some marker pens and write down on a large sheet of paper your impressions of the church in Antioch. Use single words or phrases but link them to the text of Acts. Then look at the list together and try to measure your own church alongside the picture you have drawn of Antioch. Make a second list of your own church's strengths and weaknesses as a base for mission. What do you think are the two or three most important next steps in becoming more of a missionary congregation?

2. Read aloud Acts 13.23-37. Do you agree that this is the heart of the gospel message according to Luke? Divide into pairs and explain it to one another, using your own words. Does this gospel remain at the heart of your own faith and understanding or has the good news slipped away from the centre? What can you do to recover this gospel heart?

3. Look together at the different responses to the gospel message in Pisidian Antioch and Iconium. You may want to go through the table and the text together (see above p. 15) and compare your

answers. Are there any different responses described in the rest of the Acts 13 and 14? Which (if any) describe the typical response to the gospel among the people you know who are not Christians? What other words would you use?

4. Look at the two chapters as a whole and make a list of the difficulties the apostles encountered in their missionary journey. Make a parallel list of the difficulties members of your group are experiencing at the present time in their Christian life. Where does your strength and help come from? Take some time to 'strengthen the soul of the disciples and encourage them to continue in the faith' (Acts 14.22).

5. Imagine for a moment that all the established and trained leaders in your church are taken away. How would you manage? How would you go about finding people to take on those responsibilities? What gifts do members of the group bring?

Taking action together (20 mins)

1. Write a letter to the secretary of the Church Council suggesting the two steps your church needs to take to become an effective base for mission arising from your study together of the church in Antioch and the way in which your group can help.

2. Agree to each spending time with someone you know who has drifted away from Christian faith or fellowship. Listen to the difficulties they may have experienced and seek to encourage them.

3. Take an initiative in contacting a church of another denomination in your area. Send one of your group to find out something about a church you do not know, perhaps by visiting on Sundays.

4. If you don't know already, find out what your church is doing to support mission partners overseas. Consider committing yourself to pray for them and support them in other ways.

Chapter 2
Meetings, Meetings, Meetings! – Acts 15

Conflict at the centre

Acts 13 and 14 are all action: a compressed account of what seems constant activity as the gospel takes root in Cyprus and the Roman province of Galatia. At the end of chapter 14, we expect the story to move on to the next dramatic episode of Christian expansion. But we must wait. Luke must first address the greatest conflict that affected the Early Church: how were Jewish and Gentile Christians to live together within the same community? Should the Gentiles be expected to keep the whole of the Jewish law? Or part of it (and if so, which part)? Or none at all? Those Christians who were also strict Jews governed their lives by clear rules, particularly about what they could eat and who could sit down with them to meals. How could Jews and Gentiles enjoy the full measure of Christian fellowship if they could not sit and eat together?

These issues bubble along just under the surface in the first part of Acts. In chapter 6, a dispute breaks out between the Hellenists and the Hebrews (in this case two different groups of Jewish Christians, one stricter than the other about the law). In chapter 10, Luke takes great care in telling the story of Cornelius, the first Gentile convert. At first, these individual Gentiles were exceptions to the majority of Christians.

However, as the faith expanded, more and more Gentiles joined the Church from ever more diverse backgrounds. Some had not been associated with Judaism at all before becoming Christians. In some communities, Gentiles were soon in a majority over the Jews. Within Judaism itself, Gentiles always had an inferior status even when they converted and became part of the faith. What would happen within Christianity? Some argued that the Gentile Christians should be circumcised as Jews and should be expected to keep the law. Others that neither Jews nor Gentiles were bound by the old Law of Moses.

In Acts 15, Luke tells the story of how the Early Church resolved this matter for the Church for all time and handled this difficult conflict wisely. He takes a whole chapter to deal with the matter and it is no accident that the story is told right in the middle of the book. Prior to chapter 15, Acts is the story of the Jewish Church which some Gentiles also join. After chapter 15, the Gentiles predominate, although the issue never quite goes away. Very strong passions are aroused on both sides. Luke writes as a calm historian, years after the event. As part of the study, we shall also look at a chapter of Paul's letter to the Galatians, a document written at the time of the debate, cast in much stronger and more passionate language.

The issue itself may not be a live one for us today, but the question of conflict within the Church as a whole and within the churches is all too real. The Church in history has not always been as effective as the Church in Acts in resolving issues on which Christians differ. Despite the good efforts of the ecumenical movement, the Church in the East remains divided from the Church in the West. We are better at tolerating division than at seeking reconciliation. Individual congregations, sadly, are not immune from conflict and disagreement, which can often be bitterly fought. The Church in our own day has debated and become divided over the right place for the ministry of women and continues to wrestle with issues of human sexuality thrown up by the culture around us. Conflict is part of our lives. It is not always easily resolved.

As in other sections of Acts, Luke has lessons to teach us about how to conduct ourselves when Christians disagree. We do well to take notice. The chapter also teaches us the lesson that engaging in Christian mission is not always about what happens on the front line. The whole of Acts 15 is about a series of meetings within the life of the Church, first in Antioch, then in Jerusalem, then back in Antioch again. Too many pointless business meetings can certainly lead to frustration. Yet, used rightly, these meetings can be the way to lay an even stronger foundation for the life and witness of the Christian community and have far-reaching effects. We are called to work with one another for the building of the kingdom. It is worth taking the time to learn to do that well.

Heavenly Father,
you have called us in the Body of your Son Jesus
   Christ
to continue his work of reconciliation
and reveal you to the world:
forgive us the sins which tear us apart;
give us the courage to overcome our fears
and to seek that unity which is your gift and your will;
through Jesus Christ your Son our Lord. Amen.

Common Worship: Prayer for the Unity of the Church 1

Setting the scene – Acts 15.1-5

In previous chapters we have read that the faith of the Christians in Antioch is built up by teachers who come from Jerusalem, first Barnabas and then Saul. In this chapter however, new teachers come, 'certain individuals' (Acts 15.1) and their teaching bring a great storm and disturbance to the mother church at Antioch and, by implication, to the new churches begun on the great mission of chapters 13 and 14. The message is one that does nothing less than disturb the confidence of the believers in their salvation in Christ.

The first time we hear of the teaching it is that: 'Unless you are circumcised according to the custom of Moses, you cannot be saved' (Acts 15.1). Circumcision means far more than a small, if painful, operation. In this context, circumcision was a sign that the Gentile believers would be expected to keep and to be bound by the whole Law of Moses. Salvation is both about membership of the community of faith in this life and our destiny beyond death. Enormous issues are at stake.

'Paul and Barnabas had no small dissension and debate with them' (Acts 15.2). This is Luke's civilized and understated way of saying that there was an almighty great bust up. The church in Antioch tried to resolve the matter but could not. Wisely, a decision was made to seek a resolution rather than attempt to live with permanent doubt and dissent. The new teachers and Barnabas had come from Jerusalem and it was only in that place that the dispute between them could be settled. This was no appeal for neutral arbitration but a seeking of appropriate higher authority to resolve the conflicting claims. Once again Paul and Barnabas are sent away by the church in Antioch, this time not on a mission but to resolve a question which is central to the faith they proclaim.

The long journey to Jerusalem is not wasted. On the way they 'reported the conversion of the Gentiles, and brought great joy to all the believers' (Acts 15.3). They are warmly welcomed by the church in Jerusalem. Luke mentions both the apostles and the elders who will each play a part in the debate and in the sending of the letter back to Antioch. Acts 15 is something of a bridge passage in the development of the structures of authority in the Jerusalem church. Up to this point, decisions have been taken by the apostles. In this chapter, the apostles act together with James and the elders. From this chapter onwards, it is the elders who have the responsibility of leadership. In order to resolve this key dispute, the whole range of leadership is involved and acting with a common mind. The stage is set for the debate and at the end of the introductory paragraph the point of dispute is restated, this time in Jerusalem and in slightly softer language. The issue is no longer explicitly one of salvation but we are simply told that 'It is necessary for them to be circumcised and ordered to keep the law of Moses' (Acts 15.5).

One simple yet difficult lesson from the passage is that Christians are not to avoid conflict. Striving to live in peace with one another does not mean we are called to compromise on the essential truths of our faith. Nor does it mean we should pretend our differences are not there. They need to be owned, faced and resolved. Initially this should be done face-to-face, even if it means 'no small dissension and debate' (Acts 15.2). If this proves unsuccessful, following the pattern given by Jesus in Matthew 18, we are to seek the guidance of those with greater authority in order to preserve the deeper unity of the body of Christ.

God of Barnabas and Paul,
help us and all your Church
to combine respect for all people with
passion for the truth of the gospel.
Assist us to face conflict and division
with honesty and grace,
and give wisdom to those in authority.
May we and all your people
seek to preserve the unity of the Spirit
in the bond of peace;
through Jesus Christ our Lord. Amen.

Debate in Jerusalem – Acts 15.5-21

Luke does not give us a blow-by-blow account of the Council of Jerusalem. Instead, after 'much debate' (Acts 15.7) we have three acts in what is almost a courtroom drama: evidence given by Peter, reports given by Barnabas and Paul and the pronouncing of a decision by James. Peter's speech is essentially an argument that the Gentiles have clearly received salvation without needing to keep the law. The evidence for this is the gift of the Holy Spirit and 'the cleansing of their hearts by faith' (Acts 15.9). Peter is the ideal witness to these things as it was through him that the Gentiles heard the good news. Peter also argues that even Jews must now see their salvation differently (which, by implication, puts the law in a different place in their lives): 'we believe that we will be saved through the grace of the Lord Jesus, just as they will' (Acts 15.11).

Barnabas and Paul are the next witnesses. Their testimony supports Peter's case exactly. Cornelius is not the only Gentile to have been shown God's favour. God has done signs and wonders through Barnabas and Paul as well as Peter among the Gentiles. The argument is conclusive.

The final summing up and the pronouncement of the judgement of the whole Council is left to James. This is James the brother of Jesus who is prominent in the later parts of Acts as the leader of the Jerusalem church (see Acts 12.17; 21.18; Galatians 1.19; 2.9,12). The New Testament letter of James is attributed to him. The evidence of Peter (called by his Hebrew name Simeon) finds support in Scripture. The quotation is from Amos 9.11-12 but James is drawing on a rich vein in the Old Testament of God bringing together a people for himself from the Gentiles as well as from the Jews. The momentous decision is reached on the question of salvation: '. . . we should not trouble those Gentiles who are turning to God' (Acts 15.19).

However the question remains as to whether the Gentile Christians should be given any guidelines at all by the Jerusalem church. In the event, there are four recommendations: 'to abstain from things polluted by idols and from fornication and from whatever has been strangled and from blood' (Acts 15.20). At a first reading this is an unusual group of recommendations or commandments. Some of the early manuscripts change the order or the wording here and in the letter that follows, and scholars have long debated why these four things in particular were included. The common element seems to be that the Gentile Christians are urged to have nothing further to do with pagan religion and idol worship, which was often associated with acts of sexual immorality. Even this is not made a condition of salvation however but is at the level of appropriate pastoral advice and would most certainly be helpful and essential in promoting table fellowship between the Gentile Christians and the Jewish Christians who still kept to the Law of Moses.

Note the way in which the Early Church resolves its dispute. There is no appeal here to a prophetic word or direct guidance from God. Reason, debate, the voices of experience and pastoral wisdom are seen as reliable guides for the life of the Church. The testimony of Scripture certainly forms part of the decision-making process but, in this case, it is at the end of the debate after the assembly has listened to the experiences of its members rather than at the beginning, stifling opposition and discussion.

As Luke tells the story, there is a notable absence of politics. Christians talk and listen to one another honestly, under the guidance of the Spirit, and a common mind emerges which is able to unite the assembly and which stands the test of time. Most of our church councils and committees would gain from a careful study of Acts 15.

God who knows the human heart,
you have given to Christ's body, the Church,
both authority and wisdom
to order our common life:
grant us the grace so to attend to one another,
to the Scriptures and to your gentle voice
that we may reach a common mind
and grow into a holy people,
worthy of your name;
through Jesus Christ, our Lord. Amen.

The letter to the Gentiles – Acts 15.22-35

A decision has been made but there is much still to be done. That decision must be communicated fully to those who were initially troubled by the teachers from Jerusalem. A letter alone might seem bureaucratic and impersonal. Representatives sent alone would lack the authority of the solemn Council. A letter carried by those who were themselves representatives became the favoured way of communicating in the Early Church. Most of Paul's letters were delivered by his own companions who carried other greetings and messages and were able to expand on what was unclear and strengthen the disciples.

Luke is careful to tell us that the decisions have the support of the whole Church. The text of the letter is in a different style to the surrounding chapter and it seems likely that he has copied the actual document for us: no doubt copies were made, kept and treasured by the churches in Antioch and Galatia. If that is the case, this is one of the very earliest pieces of Christian writing in existence.

The phrase 'it has seemed good to the Holy Spirit and to us' (Acts 15.28) is worth noting. Although there is no hint of a prophetic word or intervention in the debate in Jerusalem, clearly this is a decision which has become the subject of prayer just as much as the subject of testimony, well-reasoned debate and searching the Scriptures. This is a matter which has been weighed in the presence of God. For that reason, the Church can say with confidence, 'it seemed good to the Holy Spirit . . .'

Once the letter and the emissaries reach Antioch, a final meeting in the series is convened. There is much rejoicing: doubts about the salvation of the Gentiles are removed; the believers' freedom in Christ is affirmed; the way is clear to renew the mission of the churches; division has been averted. After some time, Judas and Silas return to Jerusalem whilst Paul and Barnabas remain in Antioch 'teaching and proclaiming the word of the Lord' (Acts 15.35).

There is a thread running through the chapter and the surrounding passages of the apostles seeking to strengthen and build up the life of the churches and the disciples. You may want to make a note of the different words and phrases used in the following passages:

14.22	
14.23	
14.27	
15.3	
15.32	
15.35	
15.41	
16.5	

One of the main purposes of the New Testament letters is to strengthen the churches, in a similar way to the apostles' teaching and testimony in Acts. Clearly, for the Early Church, the new Christians and the communities they formed were in need of careful nurture. The same is true, surely, for the Church in every generation, including our own. Encouragement and strength need to be intentional and come through wise and godly teaching and hearing news of what God is doing and has done in other places told by those who have been present. The Church needs both stable pastoral ministry within local congregations and those who will travel between communities, overseeing their life and spreading the news of what God has done.

A final question thrown up by the letter is one that all churches with new converts will need to address. How great a burden should we lay on the shoulders of those who come to Christ today from very different cultures to our own? What are the 'essential things' we would say that people should abstain from as young or as established Christians, either for their own spiritual health or to preserve fellowship and unity in the Church?

Prayers to be used as part of your intercessions

Lord, encourage and strengthen the churches in . . .
May they increase in numbers daily.

Lord, encourage and strengthen . . . in the Christian life.

Acts 15.32; 16.5

Acts and Galatians – Galatians 1 and 2

We have read of the founding of the churches in Galatia in Acts 13 and 14. With the controversy of Acts 15 at the front of your mind, read the first two chapters of Paul's letter to the Galatians. You may even want to go on and read the rest of the letter. The whole of this short document is an argument against the position of those advocating the false teaching that the Gentiles must keep the Law of Moses if they are to be saved.

Yet this is not a calm, orderly historian reflecting on events, but Paul the apostle, who has suffered much to bring the gospel to these churches, arguing passionately that this is false teaching and must be repudiated. We are taken now right into the heart of the debate. Evidently, the false teachers in Galatia have gained more ground than in Antioch at the time referred to in Acts 15 and the Christians there are in danger of abandoning the gospel preached by Paul, by which they were saved.

Over six chapters, Paul spells out the arguments that, no doubt, formed part of the deliberations in Jerusalem. With tender love he both rebukes them and appeals to them not to abandon their first faith in Christ.

There has been and still is considerable debate about how the events described in Acts 15 and those described in Galatians fit together. Galatians seems to be written before the Council of Jerusalem. It makes no mention of the letter sent to all the churches defining the authoritative decisions which settled the controversy (which it surely would have done). The two visits to Jerusalem referred to by Paul in Galatians can be reconciled with the visits recorded in Acts 9.26-29 and Acts 11.29-30; 12.25. The letter appears to be written from Antioch. Paul has heard news that the churches of Galatia have been troubled by the same controversies that have been stirred up in the mother church at the same time. Even Peter (or Cephas) has been disturbed from his normal practice of table fellowship with Gentiles following the visit of 'certain people from James' (Galatians 2.12). The news from Galatia may have formed part of the reason for calling the Jerusalem Council in the first place.[1]

The letter raises in a still sharper form the serious nature of the controversy. Paul uses strong language, cursing his opponents (1.9) and wishing that those who unsettle the young disciples would castrate themselves (5.12). Clearly, an enormous issue is at stake: the nature and the content of the Christian gospel of salvation. Just as Paul takes the message of the gospel seriously in his generation, so should we in our own time: taking the trouble to understand it, to appreciate its value and, if necessary, to defend it as do the apostles.

In the language of Paul and of this controversy, the message is that 'a person is justified not by the works of the law but through faith in Jesus Christ' (Galatians 2.16). In other words, the Christian faith is not about doing good things so that God will accept us, earning our salvation through works. No matter how hard we try, we cannot do this. We will always fall short. The Christian faith is about trusting that God accepts us as righteous because of Jesus Christ and his death on the cross. This is Paul's constant message in each of his New Testament letters and through the preaching in Acts. At the centre of the gospel is the message of the death and resurrection of Jesus. At the heart of our faith is salvation through faith in Jesus Christ.

The controversy that lies beneath Acts 15 and Galatians has kept on recurring in different forms all through Christian history. Men and women keep on trying to substitute the good news of the gospel of God's gift to us in Christ leading to freedom with a religion based on good works and obligations and keeping rules. Every time we hear ourselves or someone else say 'I'm not good enough to be a Christian' or 'If you were a proper Christian you would do this or that' we should beware. At the heart of our faith is the gospel of salvation as a gift to us and all the world through faith in Jesus Christ.

A verse for reflection and to commit to memory

I have been crucified with Christ;
and it is no longer I who live,
but it is Christ who lives in me.
And the life I now live in the flesh
I live by faith in the Son of God,
who loved me and gave himself for me.

Galatians 2.19-20

Farewell to Barnabas – Acts 15.36-41

At the end of the chapter which is about the resolution of conflict, it is ironic that Luke honestly records a dispute between the two companions Paul and Barnabas. The two have worked together closely until now. Barnabas has played a key role in the development of Christian mission, particularly in the church in Antioch. He is first mentioned in Acts 4.36 as one of the early Christian converts in Jerusalem. We read of his generosity, that his name is Joseph and that the apostles gave him a new name based upon his Christian character: Barnabas means 'son of encouragement' (Acts 4.36).

In chapter 9, when the newly converted Saul visits Jerusalem and the disciples are afraid of him, it is Barnabas who takes the risk and brings Saul to the apostles. In chapter 11, Barnabas is chosen as the apostles' ambassador to the new church in Antioch 'for he was a good man, full of the Holy Spirit and of faith' (Acts 11.24). Again, he encourages them: 'he exhorted them all to remain faithful to the Lord with steadfast devotion' (Acts 11.23). A great many people find faith as Barnabas shares in the leadership of the church. Barnabas' first expedition from Antioch is to travel to Tarsus and find Saul and together they engage in the work of teaching the disciples there. As we have seen, it is Barnabas who has taken the lead both at the beginning of the first missionary journey and in the Council of Jerusalem (where he is mentioned ahead of Paul in 15.12). During the journey however, it is Paul's gifts which come to prominence and it is Paul who remains in focus as we continue our journey through Acts.

The reason for the dispute between the two men who have worked together for so long and so fruitfully turns again on Barnabas' characteristic virtue of encouragement. John Mark had turned back from the first missionary journey. For that reason, Paul refuses to take him on the return visit planned in 15.36. Yet Barnabas stands by his younger companion and insists he is given a second chance (just as a younger Saul, in different circumstances was given his opportunity). The two apostles part company. Barnabas' mission continues back in Cyprus. We hear no more of him in Acts. There are hints elsewhere that the two were reconciled (1 Corinthians 9.6). The tradition tells us also that Barnabas' faith is justified. Mark was not only restored as a trustworthy companion of Paul in his later ministry (Colossians 4.10; Philemon 24; 2 Timothy 4.11) but, according to an old tradition, became the 'interpreter of Peter' and wrote the gospel that still bears his name.

Of all the characters in Acts, Barnabas is one of the most attractive and clearly defined and he is a model and inspiration to Christians in every generation. As we reflect on our own Christian lives, we may well find that God has given us friends who have been like Barnabas to us: people who have nourished our faith; encouraged our gifts; forgiven our failings and taken risks again when we have let them down. We should thank God for such people.

We should also be encouraged ourselves to look out for those whom we might befriend and build up in the Christian life and faith through our words, our companionship, through lifelong friendship so that they might become effective for the kingdom of God. In some instances, as with Barnabas, Saul and Mark, those we encourage may go on to exercise a far greater influence than we will ever have the opportunity to do ourselves because of the gifts God has given them.

Yet we should also reflect, as chapter 15 draws to a close, that those called to Christian ministry then and now are not perfect. Despite their long friendship, Paul and Barnabas are divided by a sharp quarrel. God uses their quarrel and there are now two mission teams where once there was one. Yet Luke does not disguise or condone it. Living with our own shortcomings and the faults of others is an all too real part of the Christian life.

Bountiful God, giver of all gifts,
who poured your Spirit upon your servant Barnabas
and gave him grace to encourage others:
help us, by his example,
to be generous in our judgements
and unselfish in our service;
through Jesus Christ your Son our Lord. Amen.

Common Worship: Collect for St Barnabas

Guidelines for groups (2)

Sharing together (20 mins)

1. Review together anything group members may have done as part of agreeing to take action together when you last met. Decide what you may need to do to take things forward.

2. Ask everyone to give their initial impression from reading Acts 15 and the study material. Again, share one thing you learned and one question you bring.

3. How do members of the group respond to situations of conflict? Do you run away and hide? Give in immediately? Try and mediate? Or come out all guns blazing? In the light of these readings, is any of these the right Christian response?

Studying together (50 mins)

1. As a role-play, divide into two groups. One group should argue the position of certain individuals in Antioch that all believers should keep strict rules in order to be saved. Another group should take the position of Paul and Barnabas. Anyone who wants to sit out should be the referee or the jury. Do you think this argument is really that important?

2. Read aloud the first part of James' speech (Acts 15.13-17). Reflect together on the words of Amos: 'so that all other peoples may seek the Lord – even all the Gentiles over whom my name has been called' (Acts 15.17). Can you think of other passages from the Old or New Testament that support the truth that Christianity is for all people, everywhere? Who are the people we tend to forget about today, who have become invisible to us as needing to hear the gospel?

3. 'Certain persons have said things to disturb you and unsettle your minds' (Acts 15.24). In what ways might this happen in the Christian Church today? In what ways has it happened to you? If it happens, how should other Christians respond?

4. What lessons have you learned from the study about how Christians should disagree?

5. Barnabas' character is marked by encouragement. What do you value about the gifts of the different people in your group?

Taking action together (20 mins)

1. Compose a set of four or five pastoral guidelines for adults or young people newly converted to Christian faith in your culture today

2. Think of an area in your church life where conflict may be simmering under the surface or where there are different and strongly held views. Arrange an evening where people can come together, get to know one another better and simply listen without comment to the other's point of view.

3. Write a letter of encouragement together to an individual or group. It may be someone you know personally, a neighbouring Christian congregation in difficulties, someone in prison for their faith, or a link church or mission partner in a different country. Try to 'strengthen' their faith and Christian life.

4. Make a list together of the things people say or attitudes we have that work against the central truth of the Christian gospel that we are saved by grace through faith in Christ. Agree to make small Bible text cards or bookmarks for one another as a reminder to keep this truth central to your faith.

Chapter 3
Breaking New Ground – Acts 16.1 – 18.23

New directions – 16.1-10

A new journey begins with Paul's intention to revisit the churches founded earlier but quickly expands to wider horizons as the companions find themselves travelling through Macedonia and mainland Greece. Part of Paul's calling is to preach the gospel where Christ has not been named (Romans 15.20). Throughout these three chapters, the gospel is breaking new ground. Christ has not yet been preached in Philippi, Athens or Corinth, the three cities where Luke invites us to stay the longest. We can still see the pattern of the previous journey through much of this section in that Paul normally begins with the Jewish community and only moves on when he is forced to do so. However, in several of the centres there is no existing Jewish community so new starting points must be found.

Three of the churches founded on this journey later received letters from Paul which form part of the New Testament (Philippians, 1 and 2 Corinthians, 1 and 2 Thessalonians). The Christian gospel meets a different culture again from that of Syria or of Asia Minor and the chapters see Paul preaching in Athens, the cradle of European learning and civilization.

As with the first missionary journey, it is helpful to get an overview of the three chapters by marking the route of Paul and his companions on the map either in advance or as you read Acts 16 – 18. The Bible references that refer to the journey are listed below.

- 16.1
- 16.4
- 16.6-10
- 16.11,12
- 17.1
- 17.10
- 17.14,15
- 18.1
- 18.18,19
- 18.22,23

Our starting point is Antioch and the first part is by land. The journey is once again a circle, taking in more territory that the first. This time the distance involved is about 2,600 miles (4,160 km) from Antioch back to Antioch again and the time extends to several years. 18 months is spent in Corinth alone. About half of the distance covered would be by sea. For the first time so far in Acts, the narrator presents himself as part of the group from 16.10 onwards and for much of this section. The traditional view of these passages is that either the author of Acts was present with Paul through these events or he is using a written source composed by someone who was there.[1]

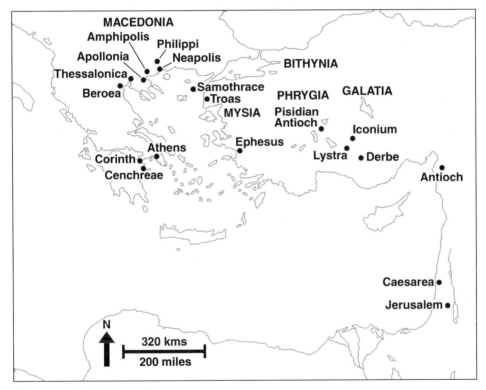

The second missionary journey

The first part of the journey is uneventful. As planned, Paul and Silas seek to strengthen the churches in Derbe, Lystra and Iconium and deliver the decisions reached in Jerusalem. Timothy joins the companions at this point. Luke gives us a picture of the churches in the region in good health with a description which is not a bad indicator for a local church today: 'strengthened in the faith and increased in numbers daily' (Acts 16.5).

However, at this point, there is a new departure and care is taken to emphasize the clear guidance of the Holy Spirit for the new period of mission which is about to begin. Two doors close and one opens. The companions have come from the east. They are 'forbidden by the Holy Spirit to speak the word in Asia' (Acts 16.6), the area to the south (although eventually their travels bring them to Ephesus). They attempt to go north to Bythinia 'but the Spirit of Jesus did not allow them' (Acts 16.7). We are not told how the companions realized they should not go south or north, simply that they are obedient to God's call. They continue to travel in the only direction open to them, to the west, and when they reach Troas, God's call is confirmed through Paul's vision in the night of a man from Macedonia.

It may be tempting to rush past these early verses to come on to the next section. Yet they are as important in their way as the beginnings in Antioch in chapter 12. According to Acts, God calls and God directs the mission of the Church and the progress of the gospel both in terms of place and of time. The travellers clearly use their heads, but remain open to the guidance of the Spirit in the strategic decisions. We will see the fruit of that in Philippi and in Corinth as, straightaway, God brings those who are ready to hear into the path of the gospel.

Again, we are led to reflect on our own call as individuals and as communities of faith. What is God saying to you, in your church, in your community? Do you sense God might be preventing you from taking some initiatives to focus on others? Where do you think God is calling you to break new ground for the gospel? Where has the ground already been prepared by the Holy Spirit?

Spirit of Jesus
you directed Paul and his companions
as they sought to preach the gospel
where none but you had gone before:
even so, inspire and guide your Church today,
help us to discern your call
and to follow boldly where you lead
for the glory of your name. Amen.

New beginnings – Acts 16.11-15

Philippi is a strategic centre for the agricultural and mining region of Macedonia: an ancient market town. It was founded as a Roman colony, with land given originally to veterans of the Roman army and was therefore the leading market town in the region. For that reason, the magistrates are very conscious of Roman law and of who may and may not be a Roman citizen (16.37). There is some speculation that it may have been Luke's home city. From Paul's perspective, Philippi is different in that it has no Jewish community: the companions need to find a new place to find those in the community who might welcome them and their message.

They find their starting point at the place for prayer and among a group of women who gather there on the Sabbath. We might suppose this to be the beginnings of a community of Jews or those interested in Judaism but it is not a strong enough gathering to form a synagogue (which needed ten men).

In Luke's gospel, Jesus gives to the twelve disciples and then to the 70 clear instructions as to what to do when bringing the good news to a new place. They are to look for those who will welcome both the disciples and their message and then stay with that person or family to establish the beginnings of a community (Luke 9.4 and 10.5-7). Jesus himself follows exactly this model when he comes to Jericho and meets Zaccheus (Luke 19.1-10), and we see Paul following similar principles in Philippi.

There is an opportunity to speak to the women gathered at the place of prayer. A wealthy business woman named Lydia is among them. 'The Lord opened her heart to listen eagerly to what was said by Paul' (Acts 16.14). She and her whole household are baptized and the opening of her heart is followed swiftly by the opening of her home, which becomes the base for the small Christian community which is swiftly established in the city (Acts 16.40).

It is no accident that the two examples of converts, Lydia and the jailer, we hear of in Philippi are a woman and a man from different ends of the social and economic spectrum. Luke is telling us clearly once again that the Christian gospel is for all people regardless of gender, class, age or racial background. Some scholars speculate that Lydia is a divorcee or a widow, which explains why she appears to be at the head of a large household.

In Philippi and elsewhere in Acts, women clearly share in the ministry and leadership of the church here from the earliest days. Paul's letter to the Philippian church singles out two women by name, Euodia and Syntyche, beseeching them to agree and bearing witness that 'they have struggled beside me in the work of the gospel' (Philippians 4.3). All manner of people are called together to live out their faith together as part of the Christian Church.

Luke places a particular emphasis in Philippi upon the way in which the Christian gospel spreads along the natural lines of existing human relationships. On two occasions he uses the word 'household', the Greek word *oikos* (16.15 and 31). In the gospel story Andrew brings Peter and Peter takes Jesus to his home; Levi is converted and invites his family and friends together for a meal. God moves in similar ways today. The word *oikos* should be taken to mean not only those with whom we live but our whole network of relationships.[2] Also in Philippi, Luke takes care to tell us of the baptism of both Lydia and the jailer with their whole household. The chapter invites us to reflect on what part our families and friends have played in our own journey to faith and the meaning
of our own baptism today.

Lord God,
we give you thanks for our families,
our colleagues and our friends.
Help us to bear witness to your love to them
in our words and through our lives.
Open their hearts to listen eagerly to your word
and to receive the good news of your Son
our Saviour, Jesus Christ. Amen.

Cry freedom! – Acts 16.16-40

Those who came to Philippi proclaiming the freedom of the gospel are imprisoned. Yet the truth of the gospel cannot be held captive and the chains and prison bars are themselves destroyed. The very jailer who fastens Paul's feet in the stocks is himself set free by Christ. The apostles are delivered from prison and, after strengthening the church, they leave Philippi and continue their mission.

The story of Paul and Silas in prison is one of the most vivid and carefully told in Acts. As we have seen, Luke is fond of drawing out parallels between Paul's experience and Peter's (the two sermons to the Jews in Acts 2 and Acts 13; the two lame men who are healed in Acts 3 and Acts 14). Here is another parallel story, to be contrasted with Peter's miraculous release from prison in Acts 12. As the story is introduced, once again Luke takes care to tell us that a civic disturbance attributed to the apostles in fact arises from good that has been done by them. They are misrepresented by their accusers who are no longer able to profit from the exploitation of a young child.

The charge against Paul and Silas is carefully recorded. Note again the enthusiasm for Roman customs in Philippi. The apostles are flogged and imprisoned yet their spirits are not quenched. At midnight, their joy is able to transcend both pain and captivity as they pray and sing hymns to God.

Luke leaves it to his readers to decide whether or not there was a direct intervention from God or whether the earthquake is simply a coincidence. There is a double ambiguity in the jailer's question: 'What must I do to be saved?' (Acts 16.30). Is he asking: 'How do I escape with my life?' or 'How do I gain eternal salvation?' Paul and Silas ensure the first by their actions and the second through their words. In a wonderful piece of symbolism, the one who washes the wounds of the apostles is then washed by them in the waters of baptism and healed from still deeper injuries. As with Lydia, it is the whole extended family of the jailer who are baptized. Experience of God's power is combined with Christian witness through the actions of Paul and Silas, with their speaking the word of the Lord and with the sacramental action of baptism.

At the end of the night, the jailer is showing to his captives a very different kind of hospitality, just as Lydia has done: 'He brought them up into the house and set food before them; and he and his entire household rejoiced that he had become a believer in God' (Acts 16.34).

In the morning the police come and order the jailer to set the apostles free but they in turn refuse their freedom. Roman citizenship is highly prized in Philippi and the magistrates now discover to their cost that they have flogged two Roman citizens. The magistrates come and apologize. Paul and Silas are still asked to leave the city, but the outcome of the incident would be to grant some measure of protection and security to the young church. We end the story where we began, in Lydia's house, which has become the centre for the new community.

We do not read of the church in Philippi again in Acts itself (apart from brief visit in chapter 20), but we can read the letter Paul wrote to the Philippians which demonstrates that a very close bond continued between the apostle and his converts here in prayer, in messages sent and in practical support:

> You Philippians indeed know that in the early days of
> the gospel, when I left Macedonia, no church shared
> with me in the matter of giving and receiving, except
> you alone. For even when I was in Thessalonica, you
> sent me help for my needs more than once
> (Philippians 4.15-16).

One of the great symbols of the Christian faith explored in this story is that of Christ bringing freedom to those who are enslaved and in prison. In what ways has that been true for you?

Long my imprisoned spirit lay
Fast bound in sin and nature's night;
Thine eye diffused a quickening ray,
I woke, the dungeon flamed with light;
My chains fell off, my heart was free;
I rose, went forth and followed Thee.

Charles Wesley

Turning the world upside down – Acts 17.1-15

From Philippi, the apostles travel south-west along the coast to Thessalonica and Beroea. Luke gives us an overview of what took place in each city focusing particularly on the different reception the gospel receives. The pattern for mission is similar to that in the first missionary journey. Evidently both of these Greek cities had substantial Jewish communities where Paul and Silas began their preaching.

The initial reception in Thessalonica is favourable. We read that some of the Jews, a great many of the devout Greeks associated with the synagogue and 'not a few of the leading women' (Acts 17.4) were persuaded and joined Paul and Silas. Luke points out yet again that the ensuing riots are not instigated by the apostles but by those who are opponents of the gospel, acting out of jealousy. The charge laid against Paul and Silas on this occasion demonstrates the reputation the Christians are beginning to attract: 'These people who have been turning the world upside down have come here also' (Acts 17.6). Again there are two meanings in the text. At one level, Luke is doing all he can to deny the charge that the Christians are causing riot and disturbance. He portrays Paul and Silas as law-abiding citizens, respectful of the traditions of others. At a deeper level, however, Luke wants his readers to understand that the reputation is a true one. In chapter 1 of the Gospel, Mary sings of the way the world is indeed to be turned upside down:

> He has brought down the powerful from their thrones,
> and lifted up the lowly;
> he has filled the hungry with good things,
> and sent the rich away empty (Luke 1.52).

Jesus teaches his disciples that in the kingdom of God, patterns of power and leadership, of wealth and poverty, of love and forgiveness, of reward and profit will all be profoundly different from those found in human society. There is a sense in which the gospel must always be turning the world upside down. If it does not, and the church blends in with the world around us, then we have lost our cutting edge and need to return to the teaching of Christ.

Beroea is not far from Thessalonica in terms of distance but the response of the people there to Paul's message was initially very different. Even so today, two communities that are close to one another physically can respond very differently to the message of the gospel. As we have seen on earlier occasions, for the Jews the touchstone of whether the gospel Paul preached was true was whether it fulfilled the Scriptures. For that reason the Beroeans take what they have heard back to the text and 'they examined the scriptures every day to see whether these things were so' (Acts 17.11).

Again we find here a rich vein of truth which runs through both the Gospel of Luke and Acts. In the stories of Jesus' birth, in the synagogue at Nazareth, in the Passion story and on the road to Emmaus, Luke demonstrates that Jesus is the one foretold in Scripture. In the preaching of Peter and Paul to the Jews, in Philip's testimony to the Ethiopian eunuch, in the response of the Jews in Beroea, those who are enquiring about Christian faith are directed to Scripture, in our context both to the Old and to the New Testament, to study and read and decide for themselves whether Jesus is the Christ.

For that reason, the Beroeans have become symbols throughout the history of the Church for Christian people who take the Scriptures seriously and study them daily with open hearts and an open mind. It is still the case that new movements, new teaching, new practice needs to be weighed and tested against the testimony of Scripture by 'ordinary' Christians as well as those entrusted with particular responsibility in the Church. The whole Church, lay people as well as clergy, needs to become familiar with the Bible, read it regularly and be able to apply what it says to our lives. Prayerful study of Scripture and action should not be separated but held together both in our lives and in the Church's mission. It is as our faith is renewed, strengthened and challenged in the reading of the Scriptures that we become, in a fuller sense, those who are turning the world upside down.

Take some time to reflect on these two things. How far does your own life and the life of the church of which you are part challenge the society around? To what extent do you and those around you know the Scriptures well enough to search them daily for the truth that nourishes our Christian living?

Almighty God,
you call your Church to be salt in the earth,
distinct from human society,
yet committed to those around us.
so nourish us through your living word
that we may be known in our generation
as those who are turning the world upside down
for the sake of your kingdom. Amen.

Preaching in Athens – Acts 17.16-34

Paul's speech to the Areopagus is one of the great moments in Acts. Speeches are very important to Luke. So is place. Acts has begun in Jerusalem. The narrative will end in Rome. At its centre, we have this symbolic visit to Athens, one of the cradles of ancient civilization and wisdom. Athens is the city of philosophy, of the sciences, of the arts and culture. By the first century, Athens is no longer a political or military force; no longer a particularly large place. But it is a place with enormous influence: a concentration of the finest minds of the time; a place with its professors and teachers; a place where the young would come to study; a place where cultures meet; a university town, famous throughout the world.

According to Acts, Paul comes to this town alone, as he comes to Ephesus two chapters later. He is greatly distressed, angered, perhaps disappointed by what he finds there. The city is full of idols. The reality is different from the reputation. As he does everywhere, Paul begins to reason ('dialogue') with the Jews and god-fearers in the synagogue. In Athens, he also takes his message out into the great marketplace, the agora, where others would be lecturing their students. As the new kid on the block, he attracts attention. The established teachers or philosophers come and debate with him: Epicureans and Stoics. They are materialists of different kinds, in stark contrast to the city around them, and the intellectual elite of a university city.

The philosophers insult Paul with their gossip and their questions: 'What does this babbler want to say?' (Acts 17.18). Then the accusation becomes more serious. 'He seems to be a proclaimer of foreign divinities' (Acts 17.18). This is a key charge in Athens because it was made against Socrates, the famous philosopher, hundreds of years previously and because of it Socrates was condemned to death. With that accusation against him, Paul has to make his plea, to justify himself before the Areopagus, the city council, where not just the governing body but many others would come to hear him. As academics they are well able to be polite but hostile at the same time. Luke writes an excellent, if caustic, description of any university: 'All the Athenians and the foreigners living there would spend their time in nothing but telling or hearing something new' (Acts 17.21).

Paul's speech in Athens is one of Luke's masterpieces, which has generated significant literature and debate in its own right. It has many layers of meaning and many subtleties of language as would be expected in classical oratory. In outline it comes in three sections.

In the first (Acts 17.22-23), Paul *connects* with his audience. Paul has used his time in Athens to soak in the concerns of the culture and to listen both to the small world in which he finds himself and to God's perspective on that world. Already in his missionary journeys we have seen how the moral and spiritual climate differs from city to city. In some it is hostile and in others welcoming. The same gospel preached by the same apostle receives very different responses. No wonder the New Testament writers see different spiritual powers or realities behind these micro cultures. As a speaker Paul finds his point of connection in the worship, which is not condemned but, in this section of the speech, affirmed. As yet, we have no deliberate confrontation, simply an invitation to listen. 'What you worship as unknown, this I proclaim to you' (Acts 17.23).

In part two (Acts 17.24-28) Paul gives his words a *context*. Greek learning, like much wisdom today, tries to explain who we are by looking at where we come from. In just a few words, Paul sketches out the story of the universe. He strikes a blow against idolatry (Acts 17.24). He strikes a blow against the religious system of the empire (Acts 17.25) in such a way that the philosophers would have to agree with him. He strikes a blow against the racial superiority of the Greeks or the Romans, which argued for different founding myths for different peoples in order to justify their superiority. And Paul affirms God's purpose in creation – the possibility open to all humanity of seeking God, reaching out to him and finding him (Acts 17.28). He ends that section by quoting the Greeks' own poets, just as the philosophers would. Just as when speaking to Jews, Paul will quote authoritatively from the Scriptures so he uses proof texts from the poets to demonstrate his argument on his audience's terms.

So far, the majority of his audience will be with him. Paul has used the city and culture around him as his starting point and visual aid. He has made the case against idolatry and temple worship in the terms that are familiar to his audience:

to the Greeks he has become like a Greek, pointing out the inherent contradictions in their position. Many in the audience will be listening hard. He has won himself a hearing.

After the connection and the context comes the *confrontation*. Without any apology or thought for the consequences, Paul proclaims the Christian gospel in all its fullness in the midst of this potentially hostile assembly.

> While God has overlooked the times of human
> ignorance, now he commands all people everywhere to
> repent, because he has fixed day on which he will
> have the world judged in righteousness by a man
> whom he has apointed, and of this he has given
> assurance to all by raising him from the dead
> (Acts 17.30-31).

Jesus is not named, yet he is present in the speech. As it does everywhere in Acts, the gospel when proclaimed immediately divides. There is controversy particularly over the resurrection. Some of them sneered. Some of them said: 'We want to hear you again' (Acts 17.32). We are told that after Paul left the council, perhaps after they had heard him again, a few became followers of Paul and believed. Dionysius, the Areopagite, certainly there for the speech, Damaris and a number of others. The challenge is at the level of the intellect. We do not read here of any signs or wonders accompanying Paul's preaching. There is not the fruit in this university city that we see in Ephesus or in Corinth among slaves and among the poor. But there is fruit and it seems at least possible that these two named converts go on to prominent ministry in the life of the Early Church.

Paul demonstrates many things in Athens: his ability to listen to the culture around him and to respond to its questions; Christianity's capacity to begin to engage the finest minds of the age; his desire to provoke public debate and comments and to see a potential audience where others would see a threat to personal safety. Most of all, however, Paul demonstrates to Christians in every generation how to speak in relevant ways to a different culture yet not compromise the heart of the Christian message: Paul in Athens calls us to be on the edge of our culture but not to sit on the fence.

Lord God, maker of the world
and everything in it,
in you we live and move and have our being:
give us wisdom both to perceive your Spirit's work
in all the nations of the world
and to proclaim with courage
the gospel of repentance and faith
in Jesus Christ, whom you raised from the dead.
Amen.

To Corinth with love – Acts 18.1-23

When I came to you, brothers and sisters, I did not
come proclaiming the mystery of God to you in lofty
words of wisdom. For I decided to know nothing
among you except Jesus Christ, and him crucified.
And I came to you in weakness and in fear and in
much trembling . . . (1 Corinthians 2.1-3).

In these words Paul was later to describe the beginning of his ministry in Corinth.
He came at a vulnerable time after a period of being persecuted and pursued from
one Greek city to another, as we have seen. He came too, possibly, shaken after
the ordeal of testimony on the Areopagus and, perhaps, disturbed by the lack of
impact his words had there.

Corinth was a great trading city: a gateway for travellers and goods between east
and west. The present Roman colony had been founded less than a century before
Paul's visit, on the abandoned site of the ancient Greek city of Corinth destroyed by
the Roman armies in 146 BC. Paul stays long enough in Corinth to establish a home,
to practise his trade of tentmaking and to lay the foundations for one of the key
churches in the region which he hopes will be a base for mission still further west.

All through the gospel and Acts, Luke sets the events he describes against the
wider background of Roman history and he do so now both at the beginning and
at the end of Paul's time in Corinth. Aquila and Priscilla have come to Corinth,
having been expelled by an edict of the Emperor Claudius from Rome. It seems
most likely that this edict can be dated to AD 49 and is the one described by the
historian Suetonius who writes: '[Claudius] expelled Jews from Rome because of
their constant disturbance at the instigation of Chrestus.' Most commentators take

'Chrestus' to be the same as 'Christ' and therefore think Suetonius is describing tensions between Jews and Christians similar to those described by Luke in Greece. Aquila and Priscilla are already, therefore, Christian ministers and Paul finds them to be congenial colleagues both here and later in Ephesus.

The mission to Corinth is similar to those described elsewhere in its strategy and Paul's movement from synagogue to an independent base in the home of one of the believers (Acts 18.7). It is marked out by its conspicuous effectiveness: a great many of the Jews and the Greeks become believers, including prominent leaders of the synagogue community. In part, this mission is so effective because Paul is able to stay 18 months rather than a few weeks or days. Luke also records the great encouragement given to Paul in a vision: 'Do not be afraid, but speak and do not be silent; for I am with you, and no one will lay a hand on you to harm you, for there are many in this city who are my people' (Acts 18.9).

Eventually, however, the Jews make a concerted attempt to disturb the young church through the legal system by appealing to Gallio, the proconsul of the province of Achaia who governed from Corinth. We know from inscriptions that Gallio was proconsul in 51 BC. For the third time in this chapter, a formal charge is brought against Paul and his companions. For the third time the charges are dismissed, this time by a very senior Roman official. The extended period of mission reflects increasing tolerance of the Christians by the Roman authorities.

The chapter reminds us again that Christian mission has at its heart the call and affirmation of the risen Christ. We are also reminded that Paul gives us a model not only for full-time ministry (for there were periods when he was undoubtedly supported by gifts from the churches) but also for Christians who support themselves by working in business or a trade but also exercise ministry in different ways within or on the edge of the local congregation. Because Paul and his companions were willing to operate in these ways, the gospel was able to expand and spread without an expensive and cumbersome structure of church government. God still calls us to be tentmakers, to break new ground and to travel light.

For reflection as you think about your own call to mission and ministry:

Do not be afraid,
but speak and do not be silent;
for I am with you,
and no one will lay a hand on you to harm you,
for there are many in this city who are my people.

Acts 18.9-10

Guidelines for groups (3)

The study section for this session focuses on the account of Paul in Philippi in Acts 16.

Sharing together (20 mins)

1. Review together anything group members may have done as part of agreeing to take action together when you last met. Decide what you may need to do to take things forward.

2. Ask everyone to give their initial impressions from their reading of Acts 16 – 18 and the study material. Which part of the passage engaged you most?

3. These are chapters of continual change and challenge. How do you cope yourself with situations of change and new directions? Ask each person to describe one such situation to the rest of the group (such as moving house, changing job, getting married or becoming a grandparent).

Studying together (50 mins)

1. Luke describes two prominent conversions in Philippi: of Lydia and of the jailer. Try and describe them in terms of opposites. List the different descriptions in the table below.

Lydia	The jailer

2. Lydia's conversion was the result of Paul and his companions seeking out the most receptive people in the city, at the place of prayer. Who are the most receptive people to the gospel in your own community? Where can they be found? What is the most helpful way to reach out to them?

3. Read again the story of Paul and Silas in prison (Acts 16.16-40). List together the people who are set free in the passage and what that freedom means to them. What does freedom in Christ mean to different members of the group (see Galatians 5.1)? How do you understand the verse from Charles Wesley (see above p. 42)?

4. Proclaiming the gospel brought continual persecution to the Early Church in many different forms (see 2 Corinthians 11.23-33 for Paul's summary). What experience have you had of suffering for the sake of the gospel? What would be the effect on your own church if you experienced a wave of difficulty and persecution?

5. Lydia and the jailer were baptized 'with their whole household' (Acts 16.15). How far has the gospel been received in your own household and network of relationships. What is the next step for you in this, as individuals and as a group?

6. What have you learned from this section of Acts about the ministry of women in the Early Church?

Taking action together (20 mins)

1. Ask two or more members of the group to find out more about a ministry that supports people in prison. Report back next time you meet to try and put into practice some kind of support for prisoners and those who work with them. You may want to lead the intercessions for your Sunday service around this theme.

2. Ask two or more members of the group to find our more about the Church in a part of the world today where Christians experience physical persecution. If you can, enter into some kind of correspondence with a Christian or church in a difficult context and seek to support them in what they do.

3. Pray together for your own household and arrange some kind of event which builds community among your network of family, friends and colleagues.

4. Find out what is happening in your church to communicate the Christian faith to those who are ready to hear more (like Lydia). Can you as a group help, support or begin this work?

Chapter 4

The Last and the Greatest – Acts 18.24 – 20.12

Setting the scene – Acts 18.24-28

The period Paul spends in Ephesus represents something of a climax to the whole of the middle section of Acts. According to Luke, these are his last years as a free missionary. The final section of the book will be taken up with the story of Paul's arrest and progress to Rome in captivity. All the lessons of the journeys in earlier chapters play their part in this third period of activity; this time not a journey so much as a settled three years of evangelism and teaching in a single strategic centre.

That centre is the great city of Ephesus, at this time the third largest in the empire after Rome and Alexandria. Ephesus was a centre of government and communication for the entire region and a centre of commerce with many coming and going both by land and by sea. It was renowned in the ancient world for the practice of magic of different kinds and, of course, as the centre for the worship of Artemis, whose temple was one of the wonders of the ancient world and whose fame was renowned throughout the empire.

Luke leaves us in no doubt, as we shall see, that the period of Paul's ministry in Ephesus was to bear enormous fruit. On several occasions he emphasizes the scale of what happened in the city itself and in its immediate region. It seems likely that teams of Paul's associates went out from Ephesus into the surrounding area to plant new churches, just as Paul himself had once set out from Antioch. As we shall see, the very economy of the region begins to be affected in different ways. Ephesus provides a base for Paul's oversight of all the churches he has helped to found from Antioch in Pisidia onwards: it sits in the centre of a semi-circle of new Christian communities.

We know that the letters we know as 1 and 2 Corinthians were written from here. Other New Testament epistles were, in all probability, written from and to this community. According to reliable tradition, in later life the apostle John was based in the church in this city. Its importance as a centre for the Christian faith in the first century cannot be overestimated. In chapters 19 and 20 of Acts, Luke lays out for us a model for Christian mission as he perceived it.

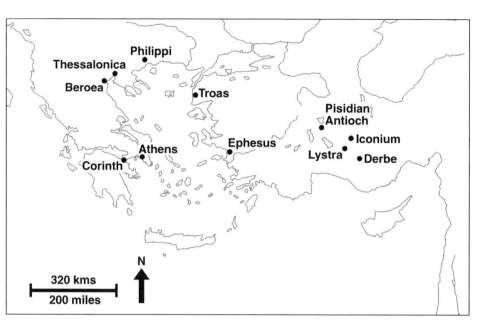

Ephesus at the centre

Yet it all begins on a very small scale. On his way back to Jerusalem from Corinth, Paul makes a preliminary visit to Ephesus and enters into dialogue with the Jews. The beginnings are promising: they ask him to stay longer. At this point, Paul declines. He moves on but clearly leaves Priscilla and Aquila there for the time being, possibly to prepare the way for a longer visit and mission on his return.

It is clear from Acts 18.24-27 that the couple continue to worship in the synagogue and dialogue with the Jews. Luke then tells us of two related incidents, the visit of Apollos and Paul's encounter with the twelve disciples in Ephesus, which give us an insight into what is happening beyond the neat borders of the main narrative. Clearly, in addition to Paul and his companions, the Early Church is engaged in a great deal more missionary activity. We have already seen how the Christian faith has reached Rome. Luke now tells us that in some form at least, Christianity has come to the Jews of Alexandria, of whom Apollos is one, and he in turn has been sent out, eager to communicate the Christian way.

At this stage in the development of Christianity, very little has been written down. There are no officially recognized 'creeds' or statements of belief and no written accounts of the life, ministry, death and resurrection of Jesus. The gospel cannot be contained, but as it spreads there is a need for the missionaries to confer together and establish that the same message is being proclaimed in very different places. This is one of the reasons why Paul takes the trouble to be in regular contact both with the 'mother' churches of Jerusalem and Antioch and with the churches he himself has helped to establish.

The Council in Acts 15 is one example of the different versions of the gospel being cross-checked against one another. We see another instance as Priscilla and Aquila listen to Apollos in the synagogue. The new teacher has much to commend him. He is 'an eloquent man, well-versed in the scriptures' (Acts 18.24). However, there are still important elements missing from his testimony. In a model of how both to correct and encourage a fellow minister, Paul's associates do not confront Apollos in public but take him aside and 'explain the Way of God to him more accurately' (Acts 18.26). His ministry thus becomes closely associated with the Pauline circle and he is sent on his way by the small group of disciples in Ephesus to build up the church in Greece, centred upon Corinth: 'for he powerfully refuted the Jews in public, showing by the scriptures that the Messiah is Jesus' (Acts 18.28).

For the small community of Christians in Ephesus, and particularly for Priscilla and Aquila, this is a season of small beginnings, of waiting and, no doubt, of prayerful preparation for the ministry that is to come. A base is being established in the community. Individuals are corrected, built up, encouraged and sent on. Perhaps a vision is growing of the mission that may develop here in God's time. The passage is of encouragement to any Christian experiencing a similar time of preparation and waiting.

Lord Jesus Christ,
you are the vine
and your Father is the vine grower:
in seasons of fruitfulness,
give us your strength and perseverance;
in seasons of pruning,
grant us patience to rest in you
and discover a deeper vision of your glory.
Amen.

Laying the foundation – Acts 19.1-7

Another consequence of the gospel spreading everywhere in such a short time was, as we have seen, that sometimes an incomplete gospel was preached and received. From time to time, therefore, the apostles need to give further instruction to particular groups of Christians. On his arrival in Ephesus, perhaps forewarned by his associates, Paul discovers one such group. In such a major centre, unlike the smaller cities in Greece, it is unlikely that Paul is the first to communicate the gospel and we see here an example of his normal practice in such circumstances.

The question Paul asks the Ephesian disciples should perhaps be seen as part of a series. In beginning a new period of Christian ministry with those who have already heard the gospel, the apostle takes great care to ensure that the existing believers are themselves fully initiated into the way. We should perhaps imagine Paul asking the church a number of questions both in public teaching and 'from house to house' (Acts 20.20) exploring their Christian faith and looking for what they need to learn.

Paul: Do you believe in God the Father who made the world?

Ephesians: Yes, Paul. We know of God the Father and we believe in him.

Paul: Do you believe in Jesus, the Messiah and Saviour of the world?

Ephesians: Yes, Paul. We know about Jesus. We know about repentance from our sins and trusting in him.

Paul: Did you receive the Spirit when you first believed?

Ephesians: No, we have not even heard that there is a Holy Spirit.

Careful questioning leads to a diagnosis that this group of disciples has not been fully initiated into the way. It is the first group in Acts to need further instruction and prayer about the Spirit (Acts 8.14-17). This in turn leads to further exploration. This group knows only the baptism of John. We know from other evidence that there continued to be followers of John the Baptist for many years after his death. The disciples are then fully initiated into the Christian way through baptism in the name of Christ. Paul lays his hands upon them and there is a mini-Pentecost at the beginning of this new period of mission: 'about' twelve disciples are filled with the Holy Spirit, speak in tongues and prophesy.

Once again, we see Luke's emphasis at the beginning of a new chapter in the story on the Holy Spirit as the one who guides and empowers the mission of the Church. Yet we see more than this. We see the importance of the full and complete initiation of the Christian community at the beginning and as part of the missionary work of the Church. For Paul to have set about preaching the gospel in Ephesus with a small but influential group of people at the core of the new community who themselves did not understand and had not experienced the full implications of the gospel would have been to build on inadequate foundations.

Throughout its history, the Christian Church has repeatedly forgotten and had to re-learn different aspects of the faith through new emphases and movements. We have seen this in recent times in the ecumenical movement; in charismatic renewal; and in the recovery of the ministry of the whole people of God. In a similar way, as individual Christians or as communities, we perhaps never learn, or we forget, something of central importance to the gospel. In those circumstances, we need to be challenged and reminded of the truths we have forgotten in order to be refreshed and renewed in our Christian discipleship. Sometimes a good place to begin in a new period of mission is the full initiation of the Church.

Luke also intends these twelve disciples to be a powerful reminder to the Church in every place and every generation of our need to experience the renewing power of the Holy Spirit in our mission. Each time the gospel is established in a major new centre, we are reminded of this dependence upon the Spirit. Time and again, this is Luke's emphasis all through Acts. The promise of Jesus (1.8); the day of Pentecost (2.1-4); Peter's challenge to the crowd (2.37-40); the believers' prayer for boldness (4.29-31); the Samaritan believers (8.14-16); the commissioning in Antioch (13.1-3): all emphasize our dependence upon the grace and power of God as we seek to engage in mission and ministry. We should pray that our own life and witness might continually be renewed by the power of God.

Send the Holy Spirit on your people.

Common Worship: Eucharistic Prayer B

Spirit of the living God, fall afresh on me.
Spirit of the living God, fall afresh on me.
Break me, melt me, mould me, fill me.
Spirit of the living God, fall afresh on me.

Paul Armstrong

The Hall of Tyrannus – Acts 19.8-10

The first part of the mission to Ephesus follows exactly the pattern established wherever there is a Jewish community: Paul continues to 'speak out boldly' and 'argue persuasively' (Acts 19.8) about the kingdom of God, continuing the work of Apollos and others. As elsewhere, everything possible is done to avoid a division in the synagogue. After three months, however, we read of the inevitable parting of the ways: 'When some stubbornly refused to believe and spoke evil of the Way before the congregation, he left them, taking the disciples with him . . .' (Acts 19.9). The rift is less dramatic than in Corinth, but, so far, there is nothing we have not read before.

It is the next part of the passage which seems to make the difference in Ephesus:

> and [Paul] argued daily in the lecture hall of Tyrannus. This continued for two years, so that all the residents of Asia, both Jews and Greeks, heard the word of the Lord (Acts 19.9-10).

In most of the other cities Paul has visited, other than Corinth, shortly after the division in the synagogue, either the Jews or some other group have stirred up so much trouble in the city that the apostle and his team have been compelled to move on. We gain a powerful insight here into the normal way the Christian missionaries operated when they were not confronted with such overt persecution.

The picture is of Paul renting a lecture hall in the centre of the city. Tyrannus was, perhaps, the owner, and possibly an early convert. One variant manuscript tradition even suggests the time for the lectures (written at the bottom of the page or in the margin of an English Bible): 'from eleven in the morning to four in the afternoon'. The pattern of Paul's day then is, we may guess, to work at his tentmaking in the morning and then over the siesta time, when people were free to come and listen, to 'dialogue' with anyone who would come and hear him each day, following the pattern of the public teachers of the day. This proves to be an enormously effective strategy when pursued over a long period of time.

This brief picture of the Hall of Tyrannus acts as a counterweight and a reminder to a number of seemingly sudden stories of conversion to Christ running through Acts. For this is a picture of the more ordinary work of evangelism and teaching in which people would come and learn at their own pace and over time. No doubt, because of their previous experience and understanding of Judaism, some would come to faith quite quickly. Others would need to be taught very slowly about the basic building blocks of faith in one God who made heaven and earth, and turning from idols, before being able to hear and understand the message of salvation in Christ. Perhaps, on any given day, there would never be an enormous crowd gathered in the hall. This is where people came to learn and to discuss, before moving on to join one of the home-based communities of Christians established in the city or back in their home town. However, the effect over time on the whole region is extremely significant.

Today, the Christian Church all over the world needs to attend to the lesson of the Hall of Tyrannus. For most people, coming to Christian faith is a journey that takes months if not years from first steps to a point of maturity.

From the time in their journey where people realize they want to know more until they are established in the faith, they need a place to come where there can be dialogue, teaching and debate about the Christian way. In Paul's words, written from Ephesus and reflecting on similar experience in Corinth, this is where the foundation is laid by the master builder for others to build on at a later date (1 Corinthians 3.10). This place needs to be outside the normal Sunday worship of the Christian communities and other gatherings for established Christians. It needs to be accessible to those who want to come in terms of time, venue and culture. Dialogue and the development of community will be as important as instruction. It needs to be regular and sustained on the part of those who offer the meeting place and teaching.

> When we contrast much contemporary evangelism with Paul's its shallowness is immediately shown up. Our evangelism tends to be too ecclesiastical (inviting people to church) whereas Paul also took the gospel out into the secular world; too emotional (appeals for a decision without an adequate basis of understanding) whereas Paul taught, reasoned and tried to persuade; and too superficial (making brief encounters and expecting quick results) whereas Paul stayed in Corinth and Ephesus for five years, faithfully sowing gospel seed and in due time reaping a harvest.
>
> John Stott, *The Message of Acts*, p. 314

Each Christian community or group of communities needs its Hall of Tyrannus as a first priority in teaching the Christian faith. Where is yours?

Almighty God,
who called your Church to bear witness
that you were in Christ reconciling the world to yourself:
help us to proclaim the good news of your love,
that all who hear it may be drawn to you;
through him who was lifted up on the cross,
and reigns with you in the unity of the Holy Spirit,
one God, now and for ever. Amen.

Common Worship: Collect for the Thirteenth Sunday after Trinity

Handkerchiefs and aprons – Acts 19.11-20

In different ways, Luke is concerned to show us that the mission to Ephesus is comprehensive, embracing every aspect of the life of the city and every part of human life. Not only do a large number of people hear the word of the Lord but, as elsewhere in Acts, the verbal testimony of the apostles is supported by miracles of healing, signs of the coming kingdom of God. This is mission in the fullest sense according to Acts. In turn we read of the way in which the gospel is established as the fulfilment of Judaism, vanquishes opposition based upon occult practices and is becoming a threat even to the most established and mainstream of the Roman and Greek gods.

In three different passages, Luke emphasizes the effectiveness of Paul's ministry in Ephesus and the scale of what was achieved. In 19.10 we read: 'This continued for two years, so that all the residents of Asia, both Jews and Greeks, heard the word of the Lord.' In this section of the chapter, following the encounter between Paul and the sons of Sceva, there is a massive public burning of magic books with a value of 50,000 silver coins. The value of a coin would be a day's wages for a labourer. Multiply the equivalent in your own currency by 50,000 to give an equivalent sum. Finally, in Luke's description of the riot, Demetrius is clear that the rise in the Christian faith is leading to an equivalent decline in business for those who sell silver statues of the goddess Artemis. Imagine the shops in your local town open but empty on a Sunday because of the effectiveness of the churches' mission in that place.

So great is the movement of the Holy Spirit in Ephesus that Paul does not have to be present even for there to be healings and deliverance from evil spirits. Handkerchiefs and aprons are carried from his workshop and lecture hall to those who are sick and suffering, presumably within the city and beyond it. They are carried by those who have faith enough and love enough to be concerned for those who are in need: a sign for us today of the value of simple acts of Christian service.

In a city where occult practices were common and regarded as nothing out of the ordinary, there was likely to be a similar preoccupation with exorcism: casting out evil spirits. All exorcism is seen by those who practise it as a confrontation between the spirit afflicting a person and a more powerful authority. Travelling exorcists, therefore, were continually seeking powerful charms and names. The itinerant Jewish exorcists attempt to use the name Jesus in prayers for those who had evil spirits but their attempt misfires and they themselves are overpowered and flee naked and wounded.

The verses remain as a warning to Christians today to be cautious about involvement in deliverance ministry which it is wisest to leave to those called to the task and given authority by the churches. Their primary message, however, is as a witness to the awesome power of God moving within that city at that time. As we recover a sense of mission in our Church today, we need a similar openness to God moving powerfully in unexpected ways in the lives of those who are coming to faith.

However, despite the widespread effects of the mission and despite the miracles of healing and deliverance, Paul's experience of ministry was never one of triumphalism or a comfortable, opposition-free ride. From Ephesus he was to write to Corinth of his difficulties and his opportunities. In 1 Corinthians 15.32 we read:

> If with merely human hopes I fought with wild animals
> at Ephesus, what would I have gained by it?

Some commentators think Paul refers to a literal encounter with animals in some kind of arena, others that he is using a graphic image to describe human persecutors who threaten his life. In the same letter he writes:

> I will stay in Ephesus until Pentecost, for a wide door
> for effective work has opened to me, and there are
> many adversaries (1 Corinthians 16.8-9).

Opposition and opportunity go hand in hand. Finally, it is to the Ephesians that Paul or one of his associates was to write the classic New Testament passage on spiritual warfare:

> Finally, be strong in the Lord and in the strength of his
> power. Put on the whole armour of God, so that you
> may be able to stand against the wiles of the devil. For
> our struggle is not against enemies of blood and flesh,
> but against the rulers, against the authorities, against
> the cosmic powers of this present darkness, against the
> spiritual forces of evil in the heavenly places (Ephesians
> 6.10-12).

The experience of the Christian life as a battle is never far away from the experience of fruitful Christian ministry.

> Be Thou my breastplate, my sword for the fight;
> Be Thou my whole armour, be Thou my true might;
> Be Thou my soul's shelter, be Thou my strong tower:
> O raise Thou me heavenward, great Power of my
> power.
>
> Irish c. 8th century, translated by Mary Byrne;
versified by Eleanor Hull

Riot in Ephesus – Acts 19.21-40

To underline this awareness of both opportunity and opposition in Christian mission, Luke now goes on to tell us of the riot in Ephesus: just as the city was to see the greatest fruit for the gospel, so it sees what was by far the biggest civil disturbance Luke records.

Before the main account of the riot, Acts 19.21-23 point us forward not only to the journeys undertaken in Acts 20 but also to the final part of Acts in Paul's remark that 'he must also see Rome' (Acts 19.21). Indeed, he is to see the city not as a free missionary but as a prisoner for the gospel. The journey through Macedonia and Achaia visiting the churches established on the second journey is undertaken both with the purpose of strengthening the churches (as Acts records) and (according to the Epistles) with the additional reason of organizing a collection from the new communities which Paul will then take as a gift to the impoverished churches in Jerusalem, strengthening the links between the two. It is for this reason, most probably, that Timothy and Erastus are sent on ahead. On this occasion, Luke chooses not to mention the collection of money: from his perspective Paul's journey to Rome has become the more important theme.

The account of the riot in Ephesus is one of Luke's most glorious set pieces of drama. The story begins and ends with two key speeches which first instigate and then disperse the rioting crowd. The first is by Demetrius. He and his colleagues appear to have been makers of small silver models of the inner part of the great temple of the goddess Artemis. Visitors to the city would buy one and take it home, not simply as an ornament but as a focus of worship in their house, enabling participation in the cult of Artemis for those unable to attend the great temple. Artemis was a goddess of fertility and of hunting, worshipped throughout the ancient world.

Demetrius makes a twofold appeal: to the loss of profits incurred by the drop in sales which he attributes to Paul's preaching and to the honour of the goddess, closely associated with the honour, influence and status of the city. Profits and patriotism are a heady mixture. Luke consistently emphasizes through the Gospel and Acts that material greed, love of money and the Christian faith do not sit easily together: a genuine response to the gospel message often means an increase in generosity. We may assume that Demetrius accurately represents at least part of Paul's message, reporting him as 'saying that gods made with hands are not gods' (Acts 19.26). We have heard this twice from Paul's own lips in Acts 13 – 20 (see Acts 14.15-17 and 17.24).

The middle section of the account (Acts 19.28-34) describes the riot itself. At the beginning and end of the paragraph, we hear the cry 'Great is Artemis of the Ephesians' (Acts 19.28), giving the impression that all of the action in between is against the background of a city in uproar with this slogan being chanted in every place. The great theatre in Ephesus has been fully excavated and, it is estimated, would hold around 25,000 people at capacity. Gaius and Aristarchus, Paul's companions, are dragged there by force. Where others would see a dangerous situation and stay away, Paul himself again sees a potential congregation and has to be restrained from going to the theatre and addressing the crowd! There is great confusion with 'some shouting one thing, some another' (Acts 19.32). A man named Alexander is put forward to speak, presumably to distance the Jewish community from the Christian proclamation, but he is shouted down with the rallying cry: 'Great is Artemis of the Ephesians' (Acts 19.34).

At length the scribe or town clerk is able to gain a hearing. He is yet another version of the official we encounter so often in Acts who does not see Christian preaching and community as a threat to civil stability. He speaks skilfully to the insecurities of the crowd: 'who is there that does not know that the city of the Ephesians is the temple-keeper of the great Artemis and of the statue that fell from heaven?' (Acts 19.35) (thought to be a reference to a meteor worshipped as a god and mentioned as an argument against the accusation that the gods are made with human hands). He dismisses the charges made against the Christians and calls for any disputes of substance to be settled in the courts. As a local man, he warns that there may be serious consequences from the commotion of the day: the Roman authorities would be aware of the riot and some would be all too ready to take away the privileges of self-government and assembly that the city currently enjoyed. The voice of reason and moderation prevails over Demetrius' radical demand for direct action.

As we read Acts today, we are again conscious of Luke's desire to defend the Christian faith against charges of riot and dissension and to assure both the Christian communities and the Roman authorities that the two can exist side by side. We also see the first significant encounter between Christian faith and the old pagan religion of the empire. Within another generation, Roman officials would begin to be more widely concerned that where the Christian faith flourished, the temples were being deserted. Within a few hundred years, Christianity had replaced the old gods as the official religion of the empire.

However, we must also be aware that underlying and within the story of Paul at Ephesus, there is a challenge to Christians in every generation that turning to

Christ also means, in many situations, turning away from the worship of other gods and (in Acts 19.18 and 19) the practice of magic and superstition. Most other religions in the ancient world allowed their followers also to worship a mixture of other gods as well as their own. Although Christianity as a whole attempted to live as far as possible in peace with Judaism and the Roman state, individual Christians were called to turn away from former allegiances as disciples of Christ. The same call is made to us today. As we respond to that call, we may in turn cause a reaction in those around us.

From the service of Holy Baptism:

In baptism, God calls us out of darkness into his
    marvellous light.
To follow Christ means dying to sin and rising to new
    life with him.
Therefore I ask:

Do you reject the devil and all rebellion against God?
I reject them.

Do you renounce the deceit and corruption of evil?
I renounce them.

Do you repent of all sins that separate us from God
    and neighbour?
I repent of them.

Common Worship: Holy Baptism

Consolidation – Acts 20.1-12

Both Luke and Paul himself now clearly believe that the mission to the area around the Aegean Sea has come to an end. Churches have been established in every major centre. From these strategic centres the gospel is beginning to spread, travelling along the natural routes of household networks and carried by teams of Paul's associates. Paul wrote to the Christians in Rome, at this time: 'so that from Jerusalem as far around as Illyricum I have fully proclaimed the good news of Christ' (Romans 15.19). Romans is written from Corinth, probably in the three-month period described in Acts 20.2, and its purpose is to prepare the way for Paul's visit to the city as part of his further ambition to be the first to preach the gospel in Spain in the most western part of the empire.

First however, there remains the task of responsible and careful consolidation work and the strengthening and encouragement of the new communities and especially of their leaders. Describing that task takes the whole of chapter 20. In the first half of the chapter we are told the route Paul followed. In the second half, we are given a concise summary of what was said not only in Ephesus but also to the elders of the churches in every place where Paul had served, as the apostle hands on his responsibilities to local ministers. As we shall see, it is Paul's purpose to found a network of Christian communities that are self-sustaining and dependent upon Christ rather than upon any human figure or universal mother church.

Luke's account of the journey is little more than an itinerary of places visited and companions. There has been some speculation that this and other similar parts of Acts are not in the form finally intended and that, perhaps, other incidents would have been inserted to give colour to the outline already written down. In particular, Luke takes no time to report the tensions between the new communities and Paul himself. We know a great deal about those tensions in regard to the church in Corinth because of the letters we know as 1 and 2 Corinthians. Nor, as we have seen, does Luke take the trouble to tell us a great deal about the collection for the church in Jerusalem which is mentioned in many of the epistles and which was clearly one of Paul's motives in travelling back to Jerusalem at this time. He refers to the gift in 24.17. The list of companions from the different churches in 20.4 may well be a list of those who were representing the different churches (see 1 Corinthians 16.3).

But, for the most part, the collection is not one of Luke's central concerns. Notice that the first-person narrator has joined the group again at Philippi. His voice has not been heard since Paul left that city and commentators assume that the source of the 'we' passages had remained in Macedonia as the companions moved on.

The story of Eutychus is told as the greatest of the 'acts' of this particular apostle during his period of free missionary activity. The story as Luke tells it is a strange mix of humour and the miraculous. We are given an insight into the normal activity of an early Christian house church: they are assembled on the first day of the week (Sunday rather than the Jewish Sabbath of the Saturday). They meet in an upper room. They break bread together. Undoubtedly there is meant to be some reference to the length of Paul's preaching here which is emphasized through Eutychus feeling drowsy, then nodding off and then, unfortunately, falling through the window.

The event itself however is turned around and becomes a resurrection miracle (parallel to Peter's raising of the widow Dorcas in Acts 9) and is told in language recalling the stories of Elijah and Elisha. Paul is at once the great worker of miracles and the object of the joke as we read that even after the event he did not stop speaking but 'continued to converse with them until dawn' (Acts 20.11)! Paul is at one and the same time the bringer of life through his preaching and life through his prayers. Yet Paul himself is not to become the object of particular veneration by later generations of Christians. He is only human (and sometimes goes on too long). We are to worship God, not ministers of the gospel.

Almighty God,
whose son Jesus Christ is the resurrection and the life:
raise us, who trust in him,
from the death of sin to the life of righteousness,
that we may seek those things which are above,
where he reigns with you
in the unity of the Holy Spirit,
one God, now and for ever.

Common Worship: Collect for the Fourth Sunday of Easter

Guidelines for groups (4)

The passage for study in this session is Acts 19.1-20

Sharing together (20 mins)

1. Review together anything group members may have done as part of agreeing to take action together when you last met. Decide what you may need to do to take things forward.

2. Ask everyone to give their initial impressions from reading Acts 18.18 – 20.12 and the study material. Which part of the passage engaged you the most?

3. Acts 19.1-20 describes the most fruitful period of three years in Paul's entire ministry. Do you believe that the most fruitful period in your life is in your past, present or future? Describe what it was (or what you hope it will be).

Studying together (50 mins)

1. 'Did you receive the Holy Spirit when you became believers?' (19.2). Is this an appropriate question for Christians to ask one another today? If not, how would you change it?

2. In what areas do you think Christians today (including yourselves) still have much to learn before we are equipped for mission?

3. There was the Hall of Tyrannus for different members of the group? Where does your Christian community provide such a place now?

4. In Acts 19.11-20, opportunity and opposition go hand in hand. Can you think of other examples of this, first in Acts 13 – 20; then from elsewhere in Scripture and finally from the experience of group members?

5. The letter to the Ephesians speaks of rulers, authorities and 'cosmic powers of this present darkness' (Ephesians 6.12). How would you describe those forces in the city of Ephesus in Paul's day? You may want to make a list on a large sheet of paper.

How would you describe similar forces in your own community and nation?

6. Is it possible to see the Church grow today in the same way it grew in Ephesus (and in Acts generally)? What needs to happen first?

Taking action together (20 mins)

1. Look at the list of what you feel you need to learn in order to be fully initiated and equipped for mission. Ask one or more of the group to do some work on how you should develop in these areas, perhaps following on from these studies on Acts.

2. Find a story of a contemporary church which is growing either in your own country or elsewhere in the world. Share the account with the group through bringing someone along as a guest, or through written testimony or email.

3. Look at your list of the forces of darkness in your own community. What practical steps forward can you take in fighting them?

4. Hold an extended time of prayer for one another and for your community. Pray especially for each member of the group to be filled with the Holy Spirit, to be able to understand their gifts and calling and to be able to bear lasting fruit in Christian ministry.

Chapter 5
Over to You! – Acts 20.17-38

Ministry in Acts – Acts 20.17-38

Christian ministry is a major theme all the way through the Acts of the Apostles. The first story told after the Ascension of Jesus is the choosing of Matthias to replace Judas. In chapter 6, Luke tells us of the appointing of the seven, as the disciples increase in number and new structures are needed. In chapter 13, as we have seen, he gives us a brief portrait of the different forms of ministry in the great sending church of Antioch. At the end of the first missionary journey, we read that Paul and Barnabas 'appointed elders for them in each church, with prayer and fasting' (Acts 14.23) on their return visits.

As with his other themes, Luke avoids repeating himself and means us to assume that this was the pattern Paul has followed consistently in the other missions described in Acts 13 – 20. Along the way, we have seen many references to Paul's co-workers, many of them drawn from the congregations he established or visited on his journeys. We have been told also of the elders in the church in Jerusalem who shared in the great Council of Acts 15 and who from that point on assume responsibility for the church there in place of the apostles.

However, little has been said so far about the role and responsibilities of these ministers in local congregations. The main emphasis in the narrative and the speeches of Acts has been upon the message preached in public to those who were being invited to join the way. At the very end of his account of the missionary journeys in this central section of the book, Luke sets Paul's speech at Miletus given to the elders of the church in Ephesus but meant as a type of the speeches of encouragement and handing on of responsibility that would have been a feature of all of Paul's return visits to the churches he founded to encourage and build up the people of God. Through Paul's words, Luke aims to address the Church of his own day and in every generation, distilling the wisdom of the first generation of Christian ministers, and especially Paul, on the nature of Christian service.

The New Testament does not give us a neat picture of the development of Christian ministry. Instead, its different strands bear witness to structures that evolved slowly according to the missionary demands of the situation. There was no blueprint from heaven. The model and example of Jesus himself was of paramount importance, particularly his emphasis on servant ministry. There was a strong emphasis running all through the tradition upon every Christian disciple exercising a ministry according to their gifts and calling.

The Early Church seems to have adopted structures for ministry adapted from the synagogues in which most of them began, with an emerging pattern of government through a group of teaching elders, the position reflected in Acts 20. By the end of the New Testament period, three words are being commonly used to describe those appointed to offices in the Church: deacon (servant); presbyter (elder) and *episkopos* (one who watches over – the word from which we take our word 'bishop'). These three words are intentionally all used in this passage by Luke (Acts 20.17,19,24,28) and they are the words which are used to carry forward the Early Church's understanding of setting apart or ordaining people to Christian ministry within the life of the Church and continue to be so used today in different ways.[1]

There has been much debate about whether Luke is describing and addressing ministers in his own day when Acts was written or reporting what might have been said by Paul. In his letters, Paul never uses the term 'elder' (or presbyter) outside the pastoral epistles of 1 and 2 Timothy and Titus and so this may be an instance of Luke reading the terms used in his own day back into an earlier period. However, Paul does use the terms 'deacon' and '*episkopos*' (Philippians 1.1) and is concerned throughout all his letters to build up, encourage and teach those charged with responsibilities of leadership and pastoral care within the new communities. The speech to the Ephesian elders is the only example of Paul's words in Acts addressed to Christians. We should not be surprised that it is the speech in Acts which most resembles the language of Paul in his letters.[2]

Whatever its origin in New Testament times, the speech has played a very significant role in the development of the Church's understanding of pastoral ministry within the local church and has been a source of inspiration and vision for that ministry in each generation. In particular, its words and phrases have been picked up in the ordination services of many different traditions as one of the earliest statements of the idea of the Christian pastoral office. For all Christian people today, the speech stands as an aid to reflection upon our own calling and ministry, particularly within the life of the local church.

Those summoned to Miletus to hear Paul were not formally ordained, as we think of that today. They were not full time but, like Paul himself, supported themselves financially as well as giving time to the care and mission of the church. They did not meet in great cathedrals but largely assembled in one another's homes around the city. They were not all formally educated but had learned what they knew by watching and listening to Paul himself and his companions.

If Paul's associates are a good guide to the composition of this group, there would be women as well as men; married and single people; different racial groups and those drawn from every section of the community: in other words a microcosm of the Church itself. Luke intends Christians in every generation to hear this speech addressed to them: a distillation and representation of Paul's own teaching on Christian ministry, itself drawn from his own practice and experience throughout the missionary journeys.

Risen Lord,
you call all your people to follow
and to serve you in our worship and our lives:
help each member of your body to discern
both our calling and our gifts
that we may offer ourselves as a living sacrifice
holy and acceptable to God
dedicated to his glory. Amen.

The Word made flesh – Acts 20.18-20 and 33-35

Christian ministry is about the people we are and the people we are becoming. It is a matter of how we live our lives and shape our character in response to God's love far more than it is about skills, actions or words. Paul begins and ends his speech with reference to the way he has modelled Christian life and ministry. The way he has lived is more important than what he has said and done and all the gifts he may have brought to his ministry: 'You yourselves know how I lived among you the entire time from the first day that I set foot in Asia' (Acts 20.18).

It is not our actions which speak louder than our words but our whole character and way of life which will commend or drown out the message of the gospel. This example means, in particular, that Paul has not engaged in Christian ministry for personal gain: 'I coveted no one's silver or gold or clothing. You know for yourselves that I worked with my own hands to support myself and my companions. In all this I have given you an example that by such work we must support the weak' (Acts 20.33-35). Although elsewhere Paul commends the practice of the Church supporting those who give their time to the Ministry of the Word, in his own pioneer ministry it is better to support himself and not be a burden to the new church than for all his time to be available. Personal gain could be extended however to embrace other things. We are called to undertake Christian ministry as servants, not in order to gain power, influence, good reputation or position.

In all of this Paul is consciously following both the words and the example of Jesus. Unusually in Acts, he quotes the words of Jesus at the end of the speech (words that are otherwise unrecorded in the gospels) much as he quotes the Old Testament Scriptures to the Jews and classical poetry to the Greeks: 'It is more blessed to give than to receive' (Acts 20.35).

At the beginning of the speech, Paul describes himself as 'serving the Lord with all humility and with tears, enduring the trials that came to me . . .' (Acts 20.19). This also is after the pattern of Christ: humility, tears and trials form a central part of Jesus' ministry. There is the implication in the speech, made explicit in Paul's letters, that as he imitates Christ, so others should pattern their lives on him:

> Be imitators of me, as I am of Christ
> (1 Corinthians 11.1).

> Keep on doing the things you have learned and
> received and heard and seen in me (Philippians 4.9).

There is something very important here about the heart of Christian ministry. As the early Christians reflected on the life and teaching and death and resurrection of Jesus, they came to realize in a fuller and deeper way that Jesus not only spoke the message of the gospel of love, but that in his life and ministry, he was that message made human. As the writer to the Hebrews puts it:

> Long ago God spoke to our ancestors in many and
> various ways by the prophets, but in these last days
> he has spoken to us by a Son, whom he appointed
> heir of all things, through whom he also created the
> worlds. He is the reflection of God's glory and the
> exact imprint of God's very being, and he sustains
> all things by his powerful word (Hebrews 1.1-2).

According to Colossians:

> He is the image of the invisible God, the firstborn
> of all creation: for in him all things in heaven and
> on earth were created . . . For in him all the fullness
> of God was pleased to dwell (Colossians 1.15,19).

The great truth of the incarnation is expressed most simply but most profoundly by the Gospel of John, using the concept of 'the Word' to capture the creative, rational, sustaining power and love of God in Greek and Hebrew thought: 'And the Word became flesh and lived among us, and we have seen his glory, the glory as of a father's only son, full of grace and truth' (John 1.14).

Paul gives us picture of Christian ministry as first and foremost living after the pattern of Christ so as to be an example to others. As the word became flesh in Jesus in a perfect way, so that power and love of God are to shape our own lives, so that others may see, albeit in a very imperfect way, some reflection of God's goodness and truth. The foundation of ministry is not, therefore, getting knowledge or skills or using gifts we have been given. The foundation of ministry is knowing Christ and being willing to be known by others. And that is something to which every Christian is called.

> Come down, O Love divine,
> Seek thou this soul of mine,
> And visit it with thine own ardour glowing;
> O Comforter, draw near,
> Within my heart appear,
> And kindle it, thy holy flame bestowing.
>
> O let it freely burn,
> Till earthly passions turn
> To dust and ashes in its heat consuming;
> And let thy glorious light
> Shine ever on my sight,
> And clothe me round, the while my path illuming.
>
> Let holy charity
> Mine outward vesture be,
> And lowliness become mine inner clothing;
> True lowliness of heart,

Which takes the humbler part,
And o'er its own shortcomings weeps with loathing.

And so the yearning strong,
With which the soul will long,
Shall far outpass the power of human telling;
For none can guess its grace,
Till he become the place
Wherein the Holy Spirit makes his dwelling.

Bianco de Siena, translated by R.F. Littledale

The tears of an evangelist – Acts 20.18-25

Paul's speech in Acts 20 has been compared to the other great 'testaments' of the Bible, the last words spoken by Jacob, Joshua, Samuel and others, and even to the last discourses of John 13 – 18. Although the scene painted by Luke does not come at the end of Paul's life, death, persecution and farewell are part of the background as, in the style of a speech near death, the apostle reviews his ministry and gives a solemn charge to his followers.

One conspicuous feature of the passage is the evidence of emotion. Tears are mentioned on three occasions (Acts 20.19,31,37), the first as part of Paul's review of his work as an evangelist not only in Ephesus but throughout the missionary journeys. The popular image of an evangelist today is in many ways the opposite of the portrait painted here. We see an evangelist, in caricature, as someone who wears a permanent smile, who uses words as their basic tool and who shows no trace of emotional vulnerability. Paul portrays his evangelistic ministry as being marked first and foremost by his example, by his vulnerability and by his suffering.

What kind of tears are shed by those who announce good news? Paul means more, I think, than weeping in response to his own suffering. Remember that Jesus said 'Blessed are those who mourn, for they will be comforted' (Matthew 5.4) not simply as a comfort to those who are bereaved but to signify that mourning is an appropriate attitude for all Christian people who have compassion for the needs of the world. How can we live in a world in which there is such suffering and not respond in the depths of our being? The tears of an evangelist are the tears of a man or woman who has listened to and perceived something of the sorrow and need in the world and who weeps, even though the same person is also called to be the bearer of good news. In order to speak the word of God to someone, usually we must first come to understand them, to know them and to be known.

Paul the evangelist reviews his method of bringing good news. 'I did not shrink from doing anything helpful' (Acts 20.20) he says, reminding us of his words in 1 Corinthians:

> To the Jews I became as a Jew in order to win Jews.
> To those under the law I became as one under the law
> . . . so that I might win those under the law. To those
> outside the law I became as one outside the law . . . so
> that I might win those outside the law. To the weak I
> became weak, so that I might win the weak. I have
> become all things to all people, so that I might by any
> means save some (1 Corinthians 9.20-22).

The speech in Acts continues on the theme of method: '. . . proclaiming the message to you and teaching you publicly and from house to house' (Acts 20.20). Two verbs are linked with two venues. Effective evangelism, for Paul, involved both the initial proclamation of the Christian message and more sustained teaching to nurture those who are new to the faith. To use the images of 1 Corinthians 3, there is milk and solid food, planting and watering, laying a foundation and building upon it. Both of these activities of proclamation and teaching were done in a public place, where anyone could come and listen. In Ephesus, as we have seen, this was the Hall of Tyrannus. However, there was also a vital role for teaching and, no doubt, proclamation, in the smaller and more private context of the household, addressing both individuals and small groups. In your own church is there both proclamation and teaching? In public and in private?

Finally, Paul reviews his message: '. . . as I testified to both Jews and Greeks about repentance towards God and faith towards our Lord Jesus' (Acts 20.21). Mark's gospel places the call to repentance and faith at the heart of the preaching of Jesus himself. Luke's language here is echoing not only the epistles of Paul but the major evangelistic calls of both Peter in Jerusalem (Acts 2.38) and Paul himself in Antioch (Acts 13.38). The reference to 'proclaiming the kingdom' (Acts 20.25) also stresses continuity with the preaching of Jesus.

In the final verses of this first part of the speech, Luke enables us to look ahead through Paul's words to the final section of Acts (21 – 28) which will trace the story of Paul's arrest in Jerusalem and his journey in captivity to Rome. The phrases in Acts 20.24 echo Paul's language in Philippians 1 and 2 Timothy 4.17. Paul must have impressed those he knew not only through his humility and compassion but also by his courage.

As we draw towards the end of a study of eight chapters of Acts which have evangelism as a major theme within them, we do well to reflect on our own experience and practice of communicating the gospel in the light of Paul's character, his methods and the message he proclaims.

For reflection

Therefore, since we are surrounded by so great a cloud of witnesses, let us also lay aside every weight and sin that clings so closely, and let us run with perseverance the race that is set before us, looking to Jesus the pioneer and perfecter of our faith, who for the sake of the joy that was set before him endured the cross, disregarding its shame, and has taken his seat at the right hand of the throne of God.

Hebrews 12.1-2

The tears of a pastor – Acts 20.25-35

Paul has faithfully discharged the responsibilities of his pastoral and teaching office. In this part of the speech he revisits this aspect of his ministry as a pastor and teacher. Again we see a reference to tears. There is no trace here of detached and dispassionate professionalism. Paul is involved with and committed to those in his care. He also recognizes that he is accountable to God, not simply to the Church, for the faithful exercise of his ministry:

Therefore I declare to you this day that I am not responsible for the blood of any of you, for I did not shrink from declaring to you the whole purpose of God (Acts 20.26-27).

Therefore be alert, remembering that for three years I did not cease night or day to warn everyone with tears (Acts 20.31).

What kind of tears are shed by those who are called to 'watch over' the flock, the Church of God? They will be tears of love and compassion, certainly. It is Paul who writes to the Corinthians: 'If I speak in the tongues of mortals and of angels, but do not have love, I am a noisy gong or a clanging cymbal' (1 Corinthians 13.1); and to the Romans: 'Rejoice with those who rejoice, weep with those who weep' (Romans 12.15).

But there is more than this. The pastoral office in the Christian Church is closely linked with that of teaching and instruction – the word translated 'warn' in Acts 20.31. To exercise pastoral care for one another is about guidance and protection as much as about presence and companionship: speaking honestly about snares, dangers and difficulties as well as words of comfort and encouragement. Exercising a pastoral and teaching ministry among those who are new to faith and growing in faith will have its disappointments as well as its joys, its heart-stretching and heart-breaking moments as well as times of enormous rejoicing.

As Paul describes pastoral ministry it is an urgent task ('I did not cease . . .'). It is a time-consuming task which cannot be confined to set days or normal working hours ('night and day'); it is a task that involves the giving of oneself ('with tears'); and it is a task that is continuous over time ('for three years').

Who is entrusted with this task? During his three years in Ephesus, Paul has clearly been concerned not simply with preaching the gospel but with shaping and building a Christian community and appointing those who will be co-workers in the task of oversight of the Church. All through Acts, one of the apostle's concerns is not to create communities that remain dependent upon those who come in from outside but to build both mature Christians and mature churches. Now, at this point in the story, Paul hands over final responsibility for the church in Ephesus to its own elders:

> Keep watch over yourselves and over all the flock,
> of which the Holy Spirit has made you overseers, to
> shepherd the church of God that he obtained with the
> blood of his own Son (Acts 20.28).[3]

The image used is that of the shepherd, which is drawn from the Old Testament where it was primarily a picture applied both to God himself (Psalms 23; 95) and to the rulers of the people (Ezekiel 34). The joy and seriousness of this pastoral calling is echoed and caught in the bishop's charge to those about to be ordained priest in the ordination service:

> Remember always with thanksgiving that the treasure
> now to be entrusted to you is Christ's own flock,
> bought through the shedding of his blood on the cross.
> The Church and congregation among whom you will
> serve are one with him: they are his body. Serve them
> with joy, build them up in faith, and do all in your
> power to bring them to loving obedience to Christ.[4]

The work of the pastor consists of both guiding and protecting the flock. We have seen something in Acts of the way in which false teachers have already come in 'distorting the truth' (Acts 15). Paul predicts (and Luke affirms with hindsight) that this will continue to be the case. Watchfulness as well as care are to be the hallmarks of the Ephesian elders and of all Christian ministers. In the biblical tradition watchfulness includes and embraces a call to pray: both interceding for those for whom we are called to care and prayerfully brooding over individuals, families and communities that we may know how best to guide and guard their faith and life. Finally, we should note that the Ephesian elders are not said to be appointed either by Paul or by their communities (though we should assume that both have been involved) but by the Holy Spirit. This is a calling given by God and empowered by the same Spirit who has empowered Paul himself.

> Almighty God,
> you have called out a people for yourself
> obtained with the blood of your own Son:
> continue to raise up among us
> those called to be pastors and teachers
> to guide and guard your flock
> for the sake of Jesus Christ our Lord,
> the great shepherd of the sheep. Amen.

The tears of a Christian community – Acts 20.36-38

For many years in much of the world the Church has evolved a pattern of church life and ministry in which the pastoral and teaching offices have been the calling of a small number of people who are able to give their whole time to the task within a single congregation. For various reasons, that pattern is now breaking down. The Church as a whole has rediscovered the calling of the whole people of God to ministry. In many denominations and places there are fewer clergy in relation to the number of churches so that, very commonly, one full-time minister will be shared between several smaller worshipping communities.

This means that, in some ways, we are returning to a situation that is not unlike that of the Early Church in Ephesus where the church in the city consisted of a large number of household-based communities, each with its own collegial group of presbyters appointed from within, exercising pastoral and teaching roles according to their gifts. These communities were linked together through the regular meeting of the presbyters, informal networking and, perhaps, through larger assemblies.

This is a picture of the Church in which a far greater number of people are called by the Holy Spirit to exercise a pastoral and teaching role as well as to play a part in the worship and mission of the Christian community. It is also a model that is much better suited to the style and needs of the Church in the present day. This does not mean that we no longer need ordained ministers who are full-time but that their role will continue to develop to include the building of community and oversight of groups of presbyters within the several churches in their charge alongside the traditional tasks of leading worship, teaching and pastoral care.

The final scene of this whole section of Acts is one of the most moving in the New Testament. It has its own authenticity. Paul and this group of elders have been through a great deal together. They have pioneered the establishing of a new community. They have shared in times of great joy and growth for the church as well as times of great trouble, danger and persecution. We are not told so directly, but it is fair to assume that they have known their share of conflict and reconciliation.

A team of ministers has grown up around Paul, who have been nurtured, trained and gradually entrusted with greater and greater responsibility. They have been leading and guiding the churches in Paul's absence as he made his final journey around the Aegean. Perhaps they had expected that, after the journey to Jerusalem, Paul would return once again to the Aegean base and that life would continue as before.

But that is not to be. Paul has told them definitively that, whilst he does not know exactly what the future holds, he knows that this must be a parting of the ways and that he will not return again to Ephesus. Final responsibility for the church is handed on to the group of elders (not to any one individual). The parting itself is an occasion for prayer and committing the young church and one another to God and also for much weeping and embracing. When we share our lives together in Christian community, deep bonds of love are formed. When those bonds are broken, through death, or change, or moving on or even through the call of God to new ministry, there is pain and emotion. Grieving (Acts 20.38) is not too strong a word for the congregation that loses a pastor or the pastor who moves on from a congregation or for any severing of the bonds of Christian community.

Yet such changes, though painful, are also occasions of growth in the Christian life and part of God's call. The Ephesian church needs to grow up into maturity, the measure of the stature of the fullness of Christ, and part of that is to let go of Paul, their founding apostle. Paul himself needs to be released for the next chapter in his own journey and ministry (even though the journey does not lead to greater fruitfulness). We know from the New Testament that both church and apostle move on to new things, following God's call. Any Christian community is a living, growing, organic enterprise. Things rarely stay the same for very long. Part of belonging to the Way is accepting that God gives to us companions and fellow-travellers for a season only here on earth. Our individual paths converge and then draw apart again as we respond to the Spirit's call. Both laughter and tears are an inseparable part of being church together.

Loving Lord,
we give you thanks and praise
for those with whom we have shared our journey
in the past and present:
those who taught us the faith
and learned it with us
those who have shared the joys and sorrows of
    the Way.
We remember those from whom we are separated
    by death (especially . . .),
entrusting them to your love.
We pray for those from whom we are separated
    by distance (especially . . .),
entrusting them to your mercy.
We pray for those from whom we are separated by
    disagreement, neglect or misunderstanding
    (especially . . .),
entrusting them to your grace.

> Look with favour on your people,
> gather us in your loving arms
> and bring us with all the saints
> to feast at your table in heaven. Amen.

The last four lines of the prayer are taken
from *Common Worship*: Eucharistic Prayer E

The message of his grace – Acts 20.32

> And now I commend you to God and to the message
> of his grace, a message that is able to build you up
> and to give you the inheritance among all who
> are sanctified.

Our journey, like Paul's, has come to an ending that is also a new beginning. We have followed the story of the gospel through the two great missionary journeys, the Council in Jerusalem and the last and greatest mission in the city of Ephesus. We have followed the story of the establishing of new churches by different means and in different places as the apostles experience failure and fruitfulness, hospitality and hostility. We have seen friendships established and also broken by disagreement and by partings and we have reflected on issues of mission and conflict, of encouragement and ministry, of change and growth, of call and ministry.

At the end of the journey, Paul commits the Christians in Ephesus, whom he loves, first and foremost to God who will not abandon them simply because the apostle is moving on. The work of the Spirit is far greater than the work of any one individual in the life of the Church. Without this great faith in the God who sustains and continues what has begun, Paul would not have been able ever to move on even from Antioch, let alone from place to place as often as he did. We perhaps need to remember Paul's example when we ourselves are reluctant to let go of a particular task or ministry.

Specifically, Paul commends the Ephesian Christians to 'the message of his grace' (Acts 20.32). The phrase is primarily a reference to the gospel message, but by extension, once again, a reference to the Scriptures which, for us, include the New Testament and the book we have been reading together.

As Christians engage with the Bible, in the presence of the risen Christ and in company with one another, it is a common experience that we are 'built up': that our faith deepens, our knowledge is extended, our friendship with God renewed, our vision of the kingdom is enlarged, our lifestyle is challenged and our call to follow Christ is refreshed and extended. That has been my own experience reading these chapters in the company of Christ, of the commentators and those with whom I have shared these studies. I hope and pray it may be your experience also and that you will continue to attend to the message of God's grace 'that is able to build you up and to give you the inheritance among all who are sanctified' (Acts 20.32).

Blessed Lord,
who caused all holy Scriptures to be written
    for our learning:
help us so to hear them,
to read, mark, learn and inwardly digest them
that, through patience, and the comfort of
    your holy word,
we may embrace and for ever hold fast the hope
    of everlasting life,
which you have given us in our Saviour, Jesus Christ,
who is alive and reigns with you,
in the unity of the Holy Spirit,
one God, now and for ever. Amen.

Common Worship: Collect for the Last Sunday after Trinity

Guidelines for groups (5)

Sharing together (20 mins)

1. Review together anything group members may have done as part of agreeing to take action together when you last met. Decide what you may need to do to take things forward.

2. Ask everyone to give their initial impressions from reading Acts 20.17-38 and the study material. Which part of the passage engaged you the most?

3. Try to sum up briefly what you have gained from the whole series of studies on Acts 13 – 20 and what you have appreciated about meeting together.

Studying together (50 mins)

1. If you had to choose a single verse from Paul's speech to sum up what he is saying which would you choose and why?

2. Summarize together (and write on a large sheet of paper) the qualities and tasks of Christian ministers in Paul's words and in his example.

3. From this passage and from your experience, who should exercise pastoral ministry in the life of the local church today – and how should it be exercised?

4. Paul's vulnerability is apparent from the references to tears throughout the speech. Can you see any parallels in the ministry of Jesus? Is vulnerability a feature of your life together as a congregation? What would be the benefits of growing together in this way? Would there be any dangers for which you would need to 'keep watch'?

5. Complete this sentence together: 'The single most important thing the Church today needs to learn from Acts 13 – 20 is . . .'

Taking action together (20 mins)

Reflect together on what you have learned from this journey through Acts 13 – 20. Then spend some time thinking about how you move on from here:

as individuals in your own Bible reading;

as individuals in your ministry;

as a group in your community life;

as a group 'taking action together'.

Liturgical Resources

This section suggests ways of incorporating the study material into the Ministry of the Word as the congregation gathers on Sundays or during the week. A short series of sermons is envisaged, one for each chapter.

For each Sunday we have provided a table of readings and very brief comments linked to material in the Church of England's *Common Worship*. There are no suggestions for music and songs because of the range of sources used by different churches.

For churches following a seasonal calendar, the material in this book is best used in Ordinary Time.

Chapter 1: There and Back Again – Acts 13 and 14

The Ministry of the Word

Jonah 1.1-17
Psalm 91.1-13
Acts 13.1-12
Matthew 28.16-20

Selecting the reading from the beginning of the passage enables the sermon to introduce the theme of the missionary journeys and this section of Acts and also to root the congregation's understanding of mission in the call of God to individuals and their response in the context of a living community of faith. The story of the call of Jonah both emphasizes that God's concern for the nations did not begin with the New Testament and offers a contrasting response to that of Barnabas and Saul. The gospel reading sets the story of Acts 13 – 20 in the context of the great commission. Psalm 91 is an appropriate prayer of blessing for those about to embark on a journey.

The prayers
The prayer 'God of grace' (p. 9) could be used in addition to the collect set for the Sunday.

The prayer 'God of the lost, the lonely and unloved' (p. 11) might be used as a post-communion prayer or as part of the intercessions.

Common Worship provides a Thanksgiving for the Mission of the Church, elements of which could be used throughout the series.

Themes for the intercessions might include prayer for the whole mission of the Church in your own country and overseas, especially for mission partners; prayers for 'prophets and teachers' within your own community; prayers that each person might hear and discern their own calling.

The dismissal of the congregation could be expanded and emphasized as each is sent out from worship to engage in God's mission to the world. One way of doing this is to use the responsorial Commission from the *Common Worship* Baptism Service:

> Will you continue in the apostles' teaching and
>   fellowship,
> in the breaking of bread, and in the prayers?
> **With the help of God, I will.**
>
> Will you persevere in resisting evil,
> and, whenever you fall into sin, repent and return to
>   the Lord?
> **With the help of God, I will.**
>
> Will you proclaim by word and example
> the good news of God in Christ?
> **With the help of God, I will.**
>
> Will you seek and serve Christ in all people,
> loving your neighbour as yourself?
> **With the help of God, I will.**
>
> Will you acknowledge Christ's authority over human
>   society,
> by prayer for the world and its leaders,
> by defending the weak, and by seeking peace and
>   justice?
> **With the help of God, I will.**

May Christ dwell in your hearts through faith,
that you may be rooted and grounded in love
and bring forth the fruit of the Spirit.
Amen.

Go in peace, to love and serve the Lord,
In the name of Christ, Amen.

Common Worship: Commission from
the Liturgy of Baptism, Dismissal.

Chapter 2: Meetings, Meetings, Meetings! – Acts 15

The Ministry of the Word

Proverbs 15.1-10
Psalm 133
Acts 15.6-21
Matthew 18.15-22

The passage from Acts captures the debate that is at the heart of the chapter and allows the sermon to develop the theme of conflict in the Christian community and/or to explore the nature of this particular conflict in the Early Church. The reading from Proverbs allows the voice of the Old Testament wisdom tradition to be heard – a tradition which undergirds the way of reaching decisions represented in Acts – and also contains an Old Testament reference to the Way. The gospel reading is about the resolution of conflict within the Church and the importance of forgiveness. The theme of the brief Psalm is the unity of the people of God.

The prayers

The collect 'Heavenly Father' (*Common Worship*: Collect for the Unity of the Church 1) could be used as an additional collect and the prayers 'God of Barnabas and Paul' (p. 25) and 'God who knows the human heart' (p. 27) could be used as post-communion prayers or as part of the intercessions.

Themes for the intercessions should include prayers for the unity of the Church and for neighbouring congregations from different churches; prayers about issues that are potentially divisive in the contemporary Church; and prayers for the healing of division within society.

As the theme of the readings is conflict within the Christian community, particular emphasis should be laid upon the Peace, perhaps by giving an extended time for greeting one another. The following might be used as an extended introduction to the Peace, with different representatives of the community reading different parts:

Christ is our peace.
He has reconciled us to God
in one body by the cross.
We meet in his name and share his peace.
Amen. Lord, have mercy.

We are the body of Christ.
In the one Spirit we were all baptized into one body.
Let us then pursue all that makes for peace
and builds up our common life.
Amen. Lord, have mercy.

Blessed are the peacemakers:
they shall be called children of God.
We meet in the name of Christ and share his peace.
Amen. Lord, have mercy.

The peace of the Lord be always with you.
And also with you.

Common Worship: Introductions to the Peace

Chapter 3: Breaking New Ground – Acts 16 – 18

The Ministry of the Word

Genesis 39.19-23
Psalm 107.1-3, 10-17
Acts 16.16-40
Luke 4.16-21

There are several possible readings from Acts in what is a very rich passage. The story of the jailer is one which can be dramatized and from which a number of very fruitful themes can be developed. The Psalm tells of deliverance from prison. The reading from the Joseph story in Genesis gives some background to the Old

Testament tradition of innocent suffering in prison and God's deliverance there. The gospel reading is Jesus in the synagogue at Nazareth declaring in the words of the Isaiah scroll that he is sent 'to proclaim release to the captives . . . and to let the oppressed go free'.

The prayers

The Collect for the Third Sunday after Trinity (*Common Worship*) resonates with the theme of freedom in Christ. The post-communion prayer for the Third Sunday before Advent (*Common Worship*) is on the theme of the kingdom and echoes some of the language of the gospel reading.

The form of intercession in *Common Worship* contains an opportunity to pray 'for prisoners and captives, for their safety, health and salvation' which might be developed further.

The account of Paul in Philippi contains, as we have seen, two references to baptism. This may provide an opportunity for the congregation to be reminded of their own baptism through the symbolism of water and the words of the service. It may also be appropriate to have an opportunity for the renewal of baptismal vows by the congregation as part of the service (see the *Common Worship* Initiation Services).

Chapter 4: The Last and the Greatest – Acts 19

The Ministry of the Word

Joel 2.23-29
Psalm 51.10-17
Acts 19.1-10
Luke 24.36-39

The Acts reading allows the sermon to develop the theme of the partial initiation of the disciples in Ephesus or Paul's missionary strategy and the Hall of Tyrannus. The other readings chosen here reflect the emphasis on the gift of the Spirit, a major theme through Acts 13 – 20. The prophecy from Joel is the one quoted by Peter in Acts 2. The Psalm is one of humility, penitence and renewal. The gospel reading is Luke's equivalent of Matthew's great commission, with Jesus' command to the disciples to stay in the city 'until you have been clothed with power from on high' (Luke 24.49).

The prayers

The Collect for the Thirteenth Sunday after Trinity is on the theme of evangelism (above p. 59 and *Common Worship*). For the post-communion prayer, the song 'Spirit of the Living God' (above p. 56) could be used, or the prayer 'Lord Jesus Christ, you are the vine' (above p. 54).

The prayers of intercession should include a particular focus on the work of evangelism in your own country, area and through your own church. Pray especially for the establishing or strengthening of the Hall of Tyrannus in your local community and for the empowering of the Holy Spirit.

It may be helpful and appropriate to offer to the congregation the opportunity to receive prayer with the laying on of hands either after the service has finished or during the administration of Holy Communion, with the particular intention of praying for renewal in the power of the Holy Spirit for the work of mission to which each is called.

Chapter 5: Over to You! – Acts 20

The Ministry of the Word

1 Samuel 12.1-18
Psalm 23
Acts 20.17-38
Mark 10.35-45

Paul's speech to the Ephesian elders is best read as a unit, although this makes
for a long New Testament reading. The Old Testament suggestion is Samuel's
'testament' at the end of his life and ministry which provided a partial model for
Luke's rendering of Paul's speech. Psalm 23, of course, picks up the shepherding and
pastoral imagery in Acts 20.28. The gospel reading explores the theme of *diakonia*,
or service, as a foundation of Christian ministry, and ministry itself as an imitation
of Christ.

The prayers
The prayer 'Almighty God, you have called out a people' (p. 78) may be suitable
as an additional collect and the prayer 'Risen Lord, you call your people to follow
(p. 71) as a post-communion prayer.

The intercessions should develop the theme of Christian ministry, taking care to
pray not only for those ordained deacon and priest but for the development of
the ministry of the whole people of God. Pray for those who exercise pastoral
ministry in formal and informal ways within your own congregation. The prayer
'Loving Lord' (p. 80) may be helpfully used at the end of the intercessions.

The service may provide an appropriate context for the commissioning of
members of the congregation to pastoral and/or teaching ministries within the
Church either with adults or with children. An appropriate point in the service
would be either after the intercessions and before the Peace or immediately
following the administration of Holy Communion.

An order of service

The following short order of service may be helpful:

Those to be commissioned stand before the congregation.

Brothers and sisters in Christ, from earliest times the Holy Spirit has called out those with particular gifts to exercise the ministry of pastoral care and teaching among the people of God and within the local church. Those who stand before us today are willing to offer themselves in this sharing in the ministry of Christ. Is it your will that we should commission them to this ministry?
Congregation: **It is.**

Will you support them and pray for them and for their families?
Congregation: **We will.**

To the candidates:
Do you believe, so far as you know your own heart, that God has called you to the work of pastoral/teaching ministry in his Church?
Candidates: **I believe that God has called me.**

Will you strive to fashion your own life and that of your household according to the way of Christ?
Candidates: **By the help of God, I will.**

Will you promote unity, peace and love among all Christian people and especially among those whom you serve?
Candidates: **By the help of God, I will.**

The minister and other representatives of the congregation pray for the ministry of the candidates in suitable words:

Keep watch over yourselves and over all the flock, of which the Holy Spirit has made you overseers, to shepherd the church of God that he obtained with the blood of his own Son (Acts 20.28).

Notes

CHAPTER 2

1. This reconstruction follows the position of Ben Witherington III in his recent commentary which contains a very full discussion of the issues, *The Acts of the Apostles: A Socio-Rhetorical Commentary*, pp. 430ff.

CHAPTER 3

1. For a full discussion see C.K. Barrett, *The Acts of the Apostles*, Vol. II, pp. xxviff.

2. The Emmaus Growth Course, *Living the Gospel*, aims to help Christians to begin to share the Christian faith with their own *oikos* or network of relationships today (available in the Stage 3: Growth book entitled *Knowing God*, The National Society/ Church House Publishing, 1996).

CHAPTER 5

1. For more on this see Steven Croft, *Ministry in Three Dimensions: Ordination and Leadership in the Local Church*, Darton, Longman and Todd, 1999.

2. Witherington gives a helpful table of references in all the epistles (p. 610) and Barrett includes a table reproducing similarities to 1 and 2 Timothy and Titus especially.

3. There has been extensive discussion of the Greek text of verse 28 which is fully discussed in the commentaries.

4. From the Ordination of Priests, *The Alternative Service Book 1980*, p. 357.

Further Reading

For those who want to explore Acts further through commentaries either because you are leading group studies or preaching, the following recent commentaries are very helpful. They are listed in order of size, readability and detail. All have lists of other books that might be consulted.

James G. Dunn, *The Acts of the Apostles*, Epworth Bible Commentary, 1996.

Ben Witherington III, *The Acts of the Apostles: A Socio-Rhetorical Commentary*, Eerdmans, 1998.

C.K. Barrett, *The Acts of the Apostles*, International Critical Commentary, T & T Clark, Edinburgh, Vol. I, 1996, and Vol. II, 1998.

Older, but still useful, is John Stott, *The Message of Acts*, The Bible Speaks Today, IVP, 1990.

Notes on the Order for Daily Prayer

Christians in every generation have found it helpful to pray and listen to Scripture using a prepared form, sometimes called a Daily Office. A very simple office is provided here for readers of this book who are not used to praying in this way and who want to set their Bible reading in the context of daily prayer.

It is helpful to find a regular time and place each day. Choose the time of day that is most convenient and helpful for you. There are six sections in each chapter and psalms are suggested for the six weekdays. The Preparation begins with a sentence of Scripture, an opening psalm and an opportunity for quiet prayer.

The Word of God suggests a psalm for each day. The psalms chosen are the Psalms of Ascents, psalms originally used by pilgrims to Jerusalem. They would certainly have been used often by Paul and his companions on the missionary journeys. There is then space to read the set Bible passage and the notes.

The prayers are in response to the Word of God. Offer your own prayers of intercession in the place suggested. It may help to keep a short list of people and situations you pray for regularly.

Most of the material here is taken from Morning and Evening Prayer in *Common Worship*. If you find this way of praying helpful, you may want to explore a more developed form of the Daily Office. One example is *Celebrating Common Prayer*, Mowbray, 1992.

An Order for Daily Prayer

Preparation

Our help is in the name of the Lord,
who made heaven and earth.

Psalm 124.8

Monday, Thursday	Psalm 24
Wednesday, Friday	Psalm 95
Tuesday, Saturday	Psalm 100

The night has passed and the day lies open before us;
let us pray with one heart and mind.

Silence is kept.

As we rejoice in the gift of this new day,
so may the light of your presence, O God,
set our hearts on fire with love for you;
now and for ever. Amen.

The Word of God

Morning by morning he wakens –
wakens my ear
to listen as those who are taught.

Isaiah 50.4

A Psalm of Ascents from the following table (using a different column week by week):

Monday	120	126
Tuesday	121	127
Wednesday	122	128
Thursday	123	129
Friday	124	130, 131
Saturday	125	132, 133

Bible reading (using the passage for the day)

Reflection on the Bible reading

Reading the notes

Prayers

The short prayer for the day (from the notes)

Intercessions are offered

The Lord's Prayer
Our Father in heaven,
hallowed be your name,
your kingdom come,
your will be done,
on earth as in heaven.
Give us today our daily bread.
Forgive us our sins
as we forgive those who sin against us.
Lead us not into temptation
but deliver us from evil.
For the kingdom, the power,
and the glory are yours
now and for ever.
Amen.

Almighty God,
we thank you for the gift of your holy word.
May it be a lantern to our feet,
a light to our paths,
and a strength to our lives.
Take us and use us
to love and serve all people
in the power of the Holy Spirit
and in the name of your Son,
Jesus Christ, our Lord.
Amen.

EMMAUS
THE WAY OF FAITH

STAGE 1: CONTACT
Ideas for meeting people where they are

If you have enjoyed using this Emmaus Bible Resource, you may be interested in *Emmaus – The Way of Faith*. This resource is designed to help churches welcome people into the Christian faith and the life of the Church.

Emmaus has three stages – contact, nurture and growth. It encourages the vision of the local church for evangelism and gives practical advice on how to develop contact with those outside the Church. The material includes a 15-week nurture course that covers the basics of the Christian life and four growth books that offer Christians an opportunity to deepen their understanding of Christian living and discipleship.

All the group notes are fully photocopiable.

The authors are Stephen Cottrell, Steven Croft, John Finney, Felicity Lawson and Robert Warren.

Visit our web site www.natsoc.org.uk/emmaus, email any enquiries to: emmaus@c-of-e.org.uk or call 020 7898 1524.

Introduction
Second edition
£4.95   0 7151 4963 6
Essential background to both the theology and practice of Emmaus and includes material on how to run the course in your own church.

Leading an Emmaus Group
£4.95   0 7151 4905 9
Straightforward and direct guide to leading both Nurture and Growth groups. It lays a biblical framework for group leadership.

Contact
£4.95   0 7151 4873 7
Explores ways that your church can be involved in evangelism and outreach.

Nurture
£17.50   0 7151 4874 5
A 15-session course covering the basics of Christian life and faith.

Growth: Knowing God
£17.50   0 7151 4875 3
Four short courses for growing Christians: Living the Gospel; Knowing the Father; Knowing Jesus; and Come, Holy Spirit.

Growth: Growing as a Christian
£17.50   0 7151 4876 1
Five short courses for growing Christians: Growing in Prayer; Growing in the Scriptures; Being Church; Growing in Worship; and Life, Death and Christian Hope.

Growth: Christian Lifestyle
£17.50   0 7151 4877 X
Four short courses for growing Christians: Living Images; Overcoming Evil; Personal Identity; and Called into Life.

Growth: Your Kingdom Come
£15.00   0 7151 4904 0
This Growth book looks in depth at two main issues, the Beatitudes and the Kingdom.

OTHER RELATED TITLES:

Praying Through Life
Stephen Cottrell
£7.95   0 7151 4902 4
Aimed at those starting out in the Christian faith and at all who find prayer difficult, or want to journey deeper in their faith.

Travelling Well – A Companion Guide to the Christian Faith
Stephen Cottrell and Steven Croft
£6.95   0 7151 4935 0
Provides instruction for important areas in Christian life such as prayer, reading the Bible, worship and relating faith to daily life. Ideal for adult Christians who are beginning the journey of faith.

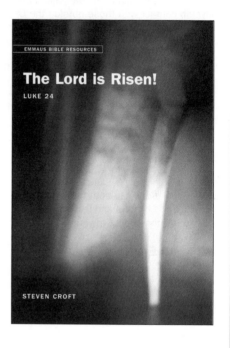